DAY TRIPS FOR CURIOUS FAMILIES

# BEND,

# OREGON

# DAYCATIONS

## KIM COOPER FINDLING

# DANCING MOON PRESS

Mt. Bachelor - dinner chairlift (Sunset)
8000 ft.
Cascade lakes - Devils - blue.
⭐Todd - 2 mile hike loop
Ale Apothecary - old brewing process in
Bend 14th St. (left)
Bug spray reminder -
IN BEND - Descute River Trail
Loop -

## Dedication

*For my mother, Joanne, for instilling in me
wanderlust, curiosity, an insatiable desire for
new experiences and a saucy sense of humor.*

# Table of Contents

Introduction                                                        7

## WEST

Cascade Lakes Highway                                              13
*Mountain lakes, ice cream cones and a ski lift to dinner*

Tumalo Falls                                                       21
*Waterfall hikes, wild beer and a flaming chicken*

Sisters                                                            29
*Western wear, folk music and a cave in a store*

Three Creek Lake                                                   37
*Alpine hikes, wildflowers and white Russians*

Suttle Lake                                                        43
*Clear waters, easy hiking and a retro-cool boathouse*

Highway 242                                                        49
*Volcanic vistas, waterfalls and hot springs*

Camp Sherman                                                       57
*Fish hatchery, country store and a river that springs from the ground*

Upper McKenzie                                                     63
*Mountain biking, lush forests and peaceful getaways*

## NORTH

Smith Rock                                                         73
*Serene spires, rail cars and buffalo nachos*

Haystack Reservoir and Lake Billy Chinook                         81
*Motorboats, rimrock views and rivers colliding*

Madras                                                            89
*Thundereggs, waterparks and alpacas*

# EAST

Pine Mountain 99
*Stars, skies and a stagecoach stop*

Prineville 105
*Rodeos, Ochocos and history*

Mitchell and the Painted Hills 113
*Layers of ash, great desserts and a bear in a cage*

# SOUTH

The Deschutes River Trail 123
*Walking, white water and marshmallows*

Lava Lands 131
*Volcanoes, ghost trees and craft beer*

Sunriver 139
*Bike trails, river access and ice cream*

Newberry National Monument 145
*Obsidian, rocky beaches and taco Tuesday*

Fort Rock 153
*High desert outposts, geological formations and dunes in the desert*

Summer Lake 161
*Hot springs, dive bars and a mosquito festival*

Crater Lake 169
*Oregon's only national park, acrophobia and a rocker on the porch*

Odell Lake 177
*A waterfall, a kokanee and a 115-year-old fireplace*

North Umpqua 185
*Waterfalls, fishing holes and river trails*

About the Author 191

# INTRODUCTION

Hey, Bend Lovers!

I know there are a few of you out there. Bend is the kind of place that inspires love. This not-so-little mountain town calls out for adoration and glorification. I've seen people develop a crush on Bend within minutes of hitting the city limits. For others it takes a little longer—maybe an entire weekend—for the adoration to stick. But this place in the center of Oregon seems to get to almost everyone after a while.

Welcome to the second edition of *Bend Daycations*. As acquainted as I am with Bend-love, I still did not anticipate how well received this book would be upon its release in 2016. In this second edition, I offer you more information, more destinations, and more to love about Bend and the places within a few hours' drive.

Maybe you've been in love with Bend for several decades or maybe your passion is new. Maybe you are a new resident or maybe you're a visitor. You've soaked up much of the fun to be had in, and immediately around, the city. You've played in the river, hit the trails, dabbled in the culture, eaten up the local foods and partied up the nightlife.

Now, you're ready for more.

You've started to wonder, what's out there? If you leave the Bend city limits, what will you discover? If you drive east, south, west, north, what will you find and what will you do there? You're ready for a day trip, and you want to know where and how to make that happen.

I am here to be your guide. I've lived in Bend for 25 years and have played here even longer. I'm a travel author, magazine editor, outdoor lover and day-trip fiend with more days exploring under my belt and more knowledge about Bend, Oregon than I can possibly keep to myself.

Who is this book for? Well, it's not for you hardcore outdoor adventurers, unless you're looking for something to do on your day off from being a badass. I will not be revealing the gnarliest canyon to kayak, the most epic backcountry ski routes, the sickest rock walls to climb or the most legit single track to tackle. I'll leave that to someone else.

This book is for you if:

- You're looking for a super fun, family-friendly, fairly mellow day trip that will likely involve nature, views, light activity and beer.
- The relatives are in town and you want to show them some sights.
- You've been in Bend for a year (or three or five) and can't believe how little you've seen outside of town.
- You have a Saturday to yourself and want to check out the Oregon Outback but are afraid of taking off with no clue what's in the outback.
- You've taken your kids to every park in Bend and can't wait to see something new but want an itinerary to guide you, including ice cream pit-stops and the best place to grab a pint at the end.
- Your curiosity has gotten the best of you and today's the day you must see the Painted Hills, but you want to know what else to do when you're out there and where the heck to eat.
- Your college friends are in town and you want to show them more than Bend's breweries.
- You're hungover and not feeling hardcore but still want to say you did something today.
- The kids desperately need to be pried out of the house and away from their iPads, but where to go?
- You're dying for an adventure, but one that doesn't

include a bike, boat, skis, lots of money or rattlesnakes.

- You like to learn a little bit about the history, natural history and trivia of where you day trip in addition to where to get an espresso or a craft beer.
- You just want to read about the wonderful, beautiful places around Bend, without actually leaving your deck chair.

If any of that sounds right, this book is for you.

The following 23 chapters are divided into four sections: west, north, east and south. I've provided some basic distance and navigation information as well as a map for each chapter, but please consult your Oregon map or smart phone before you go to get better oriented. Each chapter delivers a narrative itinerary for a day's journey, plus an additional, optional side trip and even a suggested overnighter, should your day trip extend late into the evening.

A final word to the wise: be nice to the people, flora, fauna and places you encounter. Bend and greater Oregon's popularity surge in the last decade-plus has meant an increase in use, and sometimes abuse, of this region's myriad charms. Please respect signage indicating where you should and should not park, hike, bike, picnic, Snapchat and polka dance. Plan ahead so you have what you need on your journey, make sound decisions while you are out and about, and don't take risks that result in someone having to come and rescue you. Treat the landscape with tenderness and care so that others may enjoy it for decades to come. Spread goodwill and be a good example to those in your party, and others you meet along the way.

Be a good human, have fun and get out there and enjoy your daycation!

# WEST

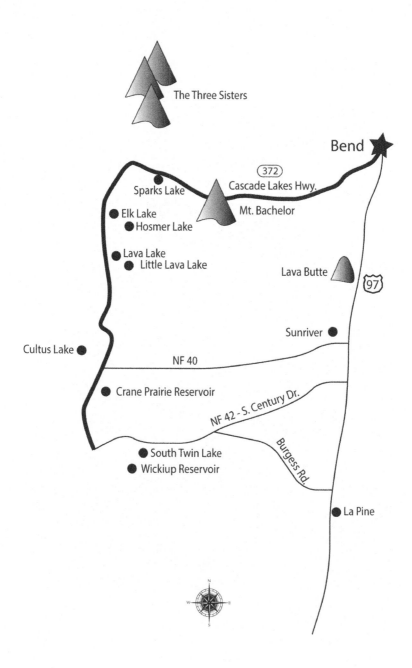

The Three Sisters

Bend

372 Cascade Lakes Hwy.

Sparks Lake

Mt. Bachelor

Elk Lake
Hosmer Lake

Lava Lake
Little Lava Lake

Lava Butte

97

Sunriver

Cultus Lake

NF 40

Crane Prairie Reservoir

NF 42 - S. Century Dr.

Burgess Rd.

South Twin Lake
Wickiup Reservoir

La Pine

# CASCADE LAKES HIGHWAY

## Mountain lakes, ice cream cones and a ski lift to a fancy dinner

*Distance: Elk Lake, the farthest destination in this day trip, is 32 miles west of Bend.*

Bend is renowned for never-ending options of outdoor glory and adventure, and Cascade Lakes Highway is its primary playground. This National Scenic Byway is so close, so easy and so rewarding. It's the first place outside of town many visitors check out, after they've explored within the city limits. And why not? Where else can you access so many beautiful lakes, beaches, trails and more, with even a resort or two thrown in to serve up ice cream and beer?

Cascade Lakes Highway is the route from Bend to Mount Bachelor, and that portion of the road is open year-round. Beyond Bachelor, the highway is gated and closed as soon as the snow gets deep, usually around November. In the winter, the journey up the hill is all about snow sports. Alpine and cross-country skiing, snowboarding, snowshoeing, snowmobiling and more are available from the highway, both before and after the gate (the only difference being, your car has to stop before the closed gate).

For summer lovers like me, winter is a waiting game for the first word that the highway has been plowed. Depending on the year, that might happen in early May, or maybe not until late June. Even after the road is cleared, there's plenty of snow on the ground in the forest and around the lakes for a while, and true summer living doesn't kick in for a bit. No matter—we all want to be up there anyway. For the handful of months of the year that the road is open, the Cascade Lakes are everyone's favorite getaway.

Mount Bachelor is 21 miles from Bend; beyond there, the road hopscotches a series of mountain lakes to the west and south. Wickiup Reservoir is the last in the line, at the far south end of Cascade Lakes Highway just past the intersection with Highway 42, which runs east/west. For this day-trip itinerary, we're going to see some sights, visit one of the more popular lakes, Elk Lake, and top off our trip with dinner on a volcano.

Packing for the lake can feel like an adventure in itself. Don't leave town without a cooler of beverages, a diversity of snacks and all your gear. What "gear" means is up to you. I'm partial to beach chairs, swimsuits, sunscreen, sun hats and a handful of issues of *The New Yorker*. If the kids are with me (and when are they ever not with me?) that list expands to include sand toys, inflatable inner tubes, maybe a Frisbee or beach ball, and more snacks. Never enough snacks. For some people, gear means standup paddle boards, kayaks, canoes, rafts, catamarans and maybe some fishing supplies. Don't forget a few layers—hopefully the day will be swimsuit-worthy, but in my experience the rule of thumb is that the Cascade lakes will be 10 degrees cooler than the temperature in town. We're heading into the mountains, after all, and as with any alpine environment, it can be windy, cloudy or even thunderstorm-y at the lakes.

The wind and thunderstorms most typically come along in the afternoon in the summer, so plan to arrive at the lake around 10 a.m. to get the most out of your day. On the way, gawk at the sights and surroundings on this amazing old highway. From town it's a steady climb to Mt. Bachelor. Just past there is an incredible view of Broken Top and the Three Sisters. Then comes a steep and winding descent past Todd Lake and Sparks Lake. At Sparks Lake, look for the pullout on the left, stop for a moment and take in the backside of the famed ski hill across the large, pretty expanse of lake and meadow. Good chance you'll recognize the vantage from many photographs.

All of these mountains are volcanoes, and the legacy of lava is everywhere. As you continue on, catch the jagged lava flow on the right of the road just after Sparks Lake and before Devil's Lake. In the mid-1960s, astronauts trained along the Cascade Lakes Highway in preparation for the Apollo missions to the moon. In 1971, Astronaut Jim Irwin of the Apollo 15 mission placed an earth rock from a volcanic dome near Devils Lake on the lunar surface. It's the only earth rock on the moon. How cool is that?

Don't miss the chance to stop, too, and see a collection of pictographs on the rocks at Devil's Lake Pass—they were painted red onto the rocks long ago. Devil's Lake is also near the trailhead that leads to the summit of South Sister, if you're wondering why so many cars are parked along the highway, or if your jam is a ten-hour hike to the tip-top of a volcanic peak. But let's not do that today—we're continuing on to Elk Lake.

Elk Lake has been a Bend getaway for nearly 100 years. A wagon road was constructed between Bend and Elk Lake in the 1920s, and shortly thereafter folks started making the journey. It's always amazing to me what early Oregonians would do for a day at the lake, in the mountains or at the shore—the thought of traveling a wagon road miles into the woods makes our 30-minute highway jaunt from town today look like a cake walk.

Elk Lake Resort is well signed from the highway. In recent years, it's gotten pretty crowded up here in high season. Come mid-week, come early in the day, or fear finding no free parking (free, as in available, and free, as in no-fee: Elk Lake Lodge sometimes charges for parking on busy days).

In Oregon, you will find, the term "resort" is used widely, and varyingly. This rustic lake lodge is not the Four Seasons, or even Sunriver, but it is a place to rent a boat and eat a burger. The lodge was built in the 1930s, shortly after the Elk Lake Guard Station was constructed (walk around the lake a short distance, clockwise, and you'll find the station and, sometimes, volunteer rangers). Today the resort is a smattering of cabins, a dock, a small store and a restaurant.

Start your Elk Lake experience on the water. It's easy to launch a boat or paddle board from the dock or beach at Elk Lake Resort. If you haven't brought your own water-going vessel, rent one. Here you can venture out a little ways or a long ways—the choice is yours. Elk is a great lake to paddle: just big enough to be interesting but not big enough to get lost on. It's usually flat enough to be safe for the kids, too, unless it's really windy. Look for wildlife: birds are overhead and on the shore, and you might even see an otter or some fish jumping. After you've had your fill of water time, return your boat to shore and get spiffed up for lunch (that means comfortable—just as it's not a fancy resort, there's no dress code here).

Elk Lake Resort is a great place to grab lunch on the deck, pick up an ice cream cone for the kids or grab a six-pack of beer if you've forgotten your local craft brew in town (though you'll pay for the oversight—six-packs aren't cheap here). Lunch isn't exactly cheap either, but it is very good—the chefs here know what they are doing and the food is tasty, especially considering you're in the middle of the woods at 4882 feet elevation. There are a handful of terrific sandwiches, and the kids will love the French fries. For you lovers of Central Oregon craft brew, you'll be glad to know the resort has generous pours of many choices of local and regional beers, served in plastic cups you can enjoy with your meal or carry down to the lower deck and sip with a great view of the dock, its collection of beautiful sailboats and the backside of Mt. Bachelor. It's lovely and tranquil.

After lunch, hit the beach. My favorite is the beach at the south end of the lake (signed from the road as simply "Beach"). There was a time when you could often have the place to yourself, and that can still happen on the occasional mid-week day. Weekends are busy, and the parking lot often fills. Please regard no parking signs and respect the native vegetation, which includes subalpine fir, lodgepole pine and manzanita, none of which enjoy being trampled by your car wheels or your feet. Though it is often crowded and can, especially late in the day, be windy, the South Beach is still a killer spot—the views are just too awesome, of South Sister, North Sister, the lake and the sandy beach before you. It's picture-perfect.

A small digression: If you get skunked at Elk Lake Resort or South Beach because everyone else got there before you, do not be deterred and head for home. There are many other lakes to enjoy up here (see sidetrip info at the end of the chapter). For experiences like Elk Lake's, with a resort serving food and beer, a beach and some equipment rentals, try Cultus Lake (15 miles south of Elk Lake) or South Twin Lake (30 miles south of Elk Lake). Cultus is popular with motorboats and has a rocky shore. South Twin is small, shallow and family-friendly, right down to the paddle boats for rent. There are other lake choices up here too; consult your map.

Now back to Elk Lake's South Beach: Set up your day camp on the east side of the beach to catch the day's latest sun; the west if you want to tuck into the trees out of the wind. There's a small trail that travels west and north around the lake to one of the lake's campgrounds—it's a fun and safe exploration for the kids. Same goes for an even smaller trail up a little knoll on the east side of the beach; it tucks into the rocky landscape and lodgepole pine that grows here, gnarled and stumpy from the wind, snow and altitude, and offers views of the lakeshore.

The lake here is shallow for a ways out, making it great for kids at play. Sometimes, there are small toads to be caught along the rocky east shore of the beach. Spend the afternoon at lake's edge, wiling away those lovely summer afternoon hours. It's always hard to leave Elk, unless the wind is whipping or the cooler's empty.

But leave you must, as your day trip isn't over—you have dinner reservations. Time your day trip to end the day with the sunset dinner at Mount Bachelor on the way back to town. It took me years to try this out and I wish I had sooner—it's an awesome experience. On Thursdays through Sundays in the summertime, Mount Bachelor runs its chairlift to the Pine Marten Lodge, where the restaurant is in full swing. Great food and cocktails are served with a killer view from nearly 8000 feet elevation.

In panorama are up-close views of the Three Sisters, Tumalo Mountain and Sparks Lake. The lodge décor and ambiance are rather mundane—it's just a ski lodge, after all—but it doesn't matter as you'll be taken with the sunset view. Descending the lift after dark is peaceful, romantic and maybe a little bit creepy depending on your fear of the dark and heights (if you've already read the Crater Lake chapter, you know I spent the descent in silent terror, white-knuckled grip on my children's collars).

You must make reservations for the sunset dinner. The menu is most often prix-fixe, and the dinner price includes a lift ticket. Take warm clothing layers—the temperature drops rapidly on summer evenings in the mountains. Return to your car with the cool of night in the mountains falling around your shoulders, and drive the steady slow descent back to Bend with the contentment of a day at the lake soaked into your soul and your bones.

## *Sidetrip*
# CASCADE LAKES

There are many other lakes on the Cascade Lakes Highway, and each is a little different and with varied charms. Little Lava Lake's claim to fame is that it's the headwaters of the Deschutes River. Wickiup and Crane Prairie Reservoirs are popular for fishing and non-developed camping, but shrink in size considerably as the summer wears on, especially in dry years (which we've had way too many of lately). Hosmer is known for terrific views, kayaking and fly fishing. Devil's

Lake is just plain gorgeous with the most amazing cerulean blue waters. Todd Lake has a trail around it and makes for a great, short 2-mile hike. Sparks Lake has great views and lots of wildflowers. Pick a new lake every weekend all summer long.

## *Overnighter*

# CAMPING

Cascade Lakes Highway is laden with awesome camping options. Many of the campgrounds fill up quickly, especially in high season. Set up camp early in the week, book a cabin at Elk Lake Resort or Cultus Lake Resort (not exactly camping but close enough in my opinion), or poke around Wickiup Reservoir for a site that isn't developed. Take the sunscreen, insect repellent, fleece jackets and marshmallows, and have fun!

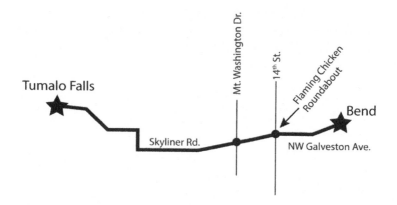

Tumalo Falls

Mt. Washington Dr.

14th St.

Flaming Chicken Roundabout

Bend

Skyliner Rd.

NW Galveston Ave.

# TUMALO FALLS

## Waterfall hikes, wild beer and a flaming chicken

*Distance: Tumalo Falls is 13 miles west of Bend.*

Tumalo Falls is Bend's backyard waterfall. Located just a hop, skip and a jump from the westside of Bend, the falls and trailhead can be reached by car by an eager explorer in under 20 minutes in summer. This accessibility makes Tumalo Falls a popular and frequent destination for Bend folk and out-of-town guests. In this day trip, we'll find some ways to linger and enjoy the area, appreciate the finer points and greater wonders of this unique ecosystem, and think about being easy on our favorite neighborhood waterfall.

Tumalo Falls is located 12 miles west of Bend at the terminus of Skyliners Road. But before you head up that one-way road, let's plan our day. This day trip is all about the outdoors, so dress appropriately for a walk in the woods in season. Also keep in mind that, like the locales off Cascade Lakes Highway, the top of Skyliners and Tumalo Falls are at just over 5,000 feet elevation, and therefore are typically a good ten degrees cooler than temperatures in town. The weather also at times moves into the Tumalo Creek canyon from the Cascade Range with a vengeance, so prepare for rain, sleet, wind, snow or hail in your wardrobe and gear pre-trip packing today.

A great stop for the day's food needs is the Village Baker, on Bend's westside. This little bakery will fuel you up with scones and sweet rolls for now, sandwiches and cookies for later.

There is even homemade blackberry iced tea and fresh-pressed espresso on hand. Fueled up and ready for take-off, now you may make your way to Skyliners Road.

The easiest way to locate Skyliners Road, aside from using your phone or car navigation system, of course, is to locate the Flaming Chicken. The name of the work of art in reference is actually "Phoenix Rising," and it flies over the center of the roundabout at Galveston and 14th Avenues. But since it was installed two decades ago, Phoenix Rising has been known by locals as the Flaming Chicken. Find the chicken, head west on Galveston, and soon enough Galveston will turn into Skyliners Road.

The road begins rising in elevation straightway, hinting at what is to come. You'll pass several schools en route west towards the forest, so please observe speed limits and watch for cyclists and pedestrians. Next up you'll pass Forest Service Road 4604 on the left, the access road to Phil's Trailhead and a huge network of mountain biking trails. Bend's mountain biking awesomeness is legendary, and can be read about in many other guidebooks, if not so much this one.

Once you pass FS 4604, Skyliners becomes pretty much an open road for ten miles. The road climbs steadily into an ever-thickening forest, with wide turns under tall trees, all of which collects plenty of snow and ice in the winter.

Speaking of winter, once upon a time, there was a ski area at the top of Skyliners Road. A group of alpine enthusiasts called the Skyliners Club founded the ski area in the 1930s, relocating their playground from their original location on McKenzie Pass. Here, in a grove of spruce and pines along Tumalo Creek, they found a location both closer to town and which provided a longer and steeper slope for toboggan runs, ski jumping and skiing. The Forest Service and the Civilian Conservation Corps (CCC) got on board, and then so did the Works Progress Administration (WPA).

A 50-man WPA crew built Skyliner Lodge (note the discrepancy in plurality—sometimes it's Skyliner and sometimes it's Skyliners; that's just the way it is around here). Built in 1935, the sturdy, rustic structure still sits at the top of Skyliners Road, just past Skyliner Sno-Park on the left. The lodge-style building of huge pine logs has been on the National Register of Historic Places since 1978 and used for a quarter of a century for conservation and outdoor education. The High Desert Education Service District maintains the site today. Take a walk up the long driveway and look at this very cool historic lodge, but don't disturb if classes (or a wedding) are taking place.

Skyliner Lodge and the ski area was the Skyliners' club headquarters through the 1940s and early 1950s, but the area was not quite high enough in altitude to provide a consistent snowpack. Then, a fire destroyed the patrol hut, tool shed, warming hut and ski tow building. The decision was clear— skiers needed a new playground. Enter, the founding of Mount Bachelor ski area, which opened to the public in 1958.

You can now guess how Skyliners Road earned its name— the club and ski area came first, eventually lending themselves to this road's moniker. Keep driving up Skyliners Road and see the sno-park on the left. Your climb has paid off; even if it didn't quite feel like it, you've gained 1,000 feet elevation from downtown Bend. In the winter, the sno-park is alive with sledding and tubing aficionados. This parking lot is also the takeoff point for cross-country skiers and snowshoers who wish to access a trail system that ventures into the woods and as far as Tumalo Falls.

In fact, the only way to access the falls in winter is on skis or snowshoes (assuming there is snow on the ground). In the summer, you can drive to the falls. Around Memorial Day, the gate that blocks winter access is opened, the road plowed, and vehicles can continue on a gravel road to the parking lot. Pay the day-use fee or display your Northwest Forest Pass, park your car and walk a short distance to an overlook. The 90-foot falls is right here before you, pouring over a basalt ledge in a shape that resembles a child's perfect drawing of a waterfall.

A brief public service announcement: Tumalo Falls can be a very busy destination because it's so close to town and so easily accessed. Please respect the delicate natural site by using designated parking spots only. Don't litter and respect signage for closed areas. If the lot is full, the site is full; come back another time. If you can, plan your visit mid-week or off-season when it's less likely to be overrun here. We want Tumalo Falls to remain the special place it is, and going easy on the land is one way to maintain the site for the future.

At the overlook, take a good look at the falls and snap all the photos you want. But don't stop there—this day trip isn't over. The real fun and the best way to experience Tumalo Falls is to ditch the crowds that gather at the overlook and take a hike up the creek. Tumalo Creek Trail is a 6.5-mile out-and-back trail that follows the creek to an amazing place called Happy Valley. Who doesn't want to go to a place called Happy Valley, I ask?

The trail is well-maintained and climbs steadily along the creek. It's uphill all the way, passing by one pretty little waterfall after the next. The beauty of the trail for those of us with kids, parents, dogs and other unpredictable beings in tow is that you can hike as short or as far a distance as you wish. Climb as much as you want or the kids will let you, take in a view or two, and turn around at any time and coast back downhill to the parking lot.

Should you continue all the way up the trail, you'll pass seven waterfalls in total. Stop for a moment in the shade, feel the breeze off the water, and take in the sights—but beware the hungry mosquitoes that have been just waiting for you to hold still so they can have a tasty mid-day snack from your flesh.

After about four miles of climbing, you'll reach Happy Valley. In the late spring and early summer seasons, hundreds of wildflowers pepper a series of idyllic alpine meadows. Look for lupine, larkspur, Indian paintbrush, columbine and more. Wooden bridges cross creeks and marshy areas. It's a little slice of wilderness heaven up here, and totally worth the hike.

Descend the trail back to the parking lot and make your

way home. As you pass through the small cluster of year-round residences just below the sno-park, your phone map might pick up a place bearing a curious name, located in one of the structures along the creek. What is The Ale Apothecary, you wonder? The Ale Apothecary is one of Bend's many craft breweries, though it might qualify as the most unique of the bunch. Paul Arney started his tiny brewery here in the woods in 2011, with a goal to tie the beer and brewery directly to the land. Using water from the ground and capturing wild airborne yeasts, the Ale Apothecary makes beer without any of the modern processes you'll find down in town.

While it's great fun to think about the beer being made right here from the fresh air and natural products of these magical woods you've been traipsing through, don't go knocking on this door. The brewery location here on Skyliners Road is not open to the public. Don't worry—Ale Apothecary beers are still in your very near future on this day trip.

Travel Skyliners Road back into Bend and take a right at the Flaming Chicken. The Ale Apothecary Tasting Room is about a mile south on 14th Street on the left. Belly up to the very small bar and taste a barrel-aged sour made in the woods you just visited. Sip on a Farmhouse Ale or the Sahalie. Taste a bit of the forest you've just spent the day in. Ahhhh.

## *Sidetrip*
## BRIDGE CREEK

Bridge Creek flows from the mountains and feeds into Tumalo Creek, right below the falls. Aside from being another gorgeous, wooded creek with trails and forest to explore not too far from town, Bridge Creek holds the distinction of being Bend's primary municipal water source. Because of this, to protect the drinking water, the Bend Municipal Watershed and the Bridge Creek Trail are closed to bikes, dogs, horses, camping and all fires. For some of us, these might be advantages. Take a walk amongst only other humans, and take a moment to appreciate the delicious, clean water Bend is known for while you are at it.

A second super cool way to appreciate Bridge Creek and Tumalo Creek is to summit Tumalo Mountain, which is accessed via the Cascade Lakes Highway and sits just on the other side of the road from Mount Bachelor. Tumalo Mountain is a steep, short climb (two miles to the top) with a great payoff of 360-degree views of the Cascade Range. From the summit, look to the northeast, and you'll be peering down into the Tumalo Creek and Bridge Creek canyons and watersheds. Here is your birds-eye view of Happy Valley. It's a really awesome perspective to compare to the hike up the creek to the valley you did another day.

## *Overnighter*
## TUMALO STATE PARK

"Tumalo" is a common place name around Bend. There are Tumalo Creek and Falls, the areas located west of Bend up Skyliners Road that we discussed in this chapter. There is Tumalo Mountain, up Cascade Lakes Highway near Mount Bachelor, mentioned above. There is Tumalo, the farming and ranching community, located northwest of Bend, en route to Sisters. These places are not exactly located adjacent to one another, you might notice. Further adding to the confusion is Tumalo State Park, located on the Deschutes River near, but not exactly in, Tumalo the community. All naming parameters and potential confusions notwithstanding, Tumalo State Park is a wonderful multi-use site with lots of great campsites, yurts and RV sites for overnight stays. There is a day-use area with river access, picnic areas, and pretty rimrock walls as scenery. Book a site and spend the night at one of Bend's many places named Tumalo.

# TUMALO FALLS

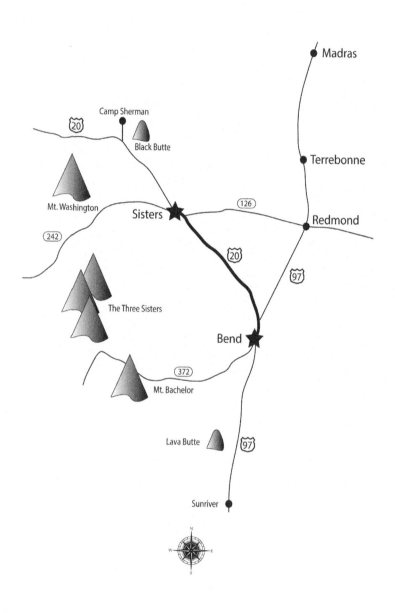

# SISTERS

## Western wear, folk music and a cave in a store

*Distance: Sisters is 23 miles northwest of Bend.*

The town of Sisters holds a funny mystique in Central Oregon. If you feel like you haven't quite figured out the small town located northwest of Bend, you're not alone. Is it an authentic Western outpost; a smart, artsy community; a kitschy tourist destination; or simply somewhere to drive through to get to the Valley or the coast? Perhaps more confusing is that, depending on who you're talking to, you might hear Sisters lauded or derided in equal parts. The truth is, Sisters is a little bit of all of the things it is accused of being. But it has great charms if you know what to look for—and when to visit.

The first thing to know is what Sisters does well. Second to Western charm, this town thrives on events. From classic cars to antiques to quilts to music to a yee-haw of a rodeo, Sisters has created an event to celebrate it. Considering that a majority of these events take place during the high season—June through September—summer brings much hustle and bustle to choose from, within a short amount of time. The rest of the year, Sisters is often as sleepy as a baby. This fact alone is at the heart of the laud/deride conundrum surrounding Sisters—in the summer, it's really busy here. Therefore, when to visit has a lot to do with how you feel about hustle, bustle and crowds.

The largest event of the year is the Sisters Quilt Show, held each July. The biggest outdoor quilt show in the world displays

1300 gorgeous handmade quilts around town, and draws 10,000 people from all 50 states and many foreign countries. These latter facts are precisely why I've never actually been to the Sisters Quilt Show. As awesome as this event purportedly is, I don't want to hang out with 10,000 people unless I'm at a Taylor Swift concert.

Since you're stuck with me as your guide, you're not going to the Sisters Quilt Show either. (However, your mother will love it.) We're going to plan this day trip around another Sisters event, one I do enjoy, the Sisters Folk Festival. But if you're just not an event person at all, or COVID-19 or some variant is still ruining events for all time, take the same trip I outline here on any quiet Tuesday or off-season Saturday—you'll still experience the high points of this Sisters city tour.

Sisters is 20 miles west and north of Bend on Highway 22. No need to pack anything for this journey but layers of clothing and cash. Maybe take a blanket if you want to sit in the park for a while. Park your car near Village Green City Park, headquarters for the main event venues for the Sisters Folk Festival.

The Sisters Folk Festival takes place the weekend after Labor Day each year. If you want to enter the tent and hear the music in the traditional up-close way, you'll need to buy tickets far in advance (this event sells out early). Alternatively, be a lurker. Spend as long as you want hanging out in Village Green Park. There is a great play structure, a clean restroom, and the kids can frolic and make new friends while you listen to the sounds of the music coming from inside the tent and take in the people watching. There are food booths set up in the park, so it's easy to grab something to eat and kick back on the grass or at a picnic table.

When the kids get restless or you do, it's time for a walkabout. September is my favorite month in Central Oregon—the weather is simply perfect, usually in the 70s, but crowds thin, making it the perfect time to explore both city and countryside. Sisters is great for strolling because it's compact—from the park you can walk almost everywhere. We're going to do a little strolling and shopping, with more music, too.

Start your journey by heading north a block and west two blocks to the Sisters Coffee Company for some refreshment. This grand log building takes the Sisters Western theme to the max. Look for horseshoes, rope and lots of wrought iron. Right across the street is Paulina Springs Books, a terrific little bookstore with a great selection of local, kid and adult reads, as well as gifts.

Turn north on Oak, maybe venturing into two Sisters institutions. Beacham's Clocks is an awesome old-fashioned clock gallery and repair shop. It's worth a peek just to hear all of those gorgeous clocks ticking away. Owner Ed Beacham has been doing this for a long time and will be happy to talk to you about the clocks. At West Cascade Avenue—the main drag through town—you'll pass The Stitchin Post, the fabric and quilting shop that is the origin story of the Quilt Show. It's not unlike the clock shop in authenticity and aesthetic pleasure, and even if you are worthless with a needle and thread, it's fun to stop in this shop to take in the colors and sights of so many beautiful fabrics. (Your mother will love it.)

While we're on West Cascade, which is also Highway 20, a word about the look and feel of Sisters. It's not an accident that this town looks like a set out of a Western movie. In 1978, the town passed an ordinance requiring 1880s-style storefronts. It was just a few years after the establishment of Black Butte Ranch, and developer Brooks Resources suggested that a theme for Sisters might boost visitation to the small city. The rest, as they say, is history. Or simulated history, anyway.

Keep walking north, avoiding the crowds and traffic of the main street, and take a right on West Main. The Folk Festival has several additional venues in addition to the park. Angeline's Bakery is one of these, as well as a great spot for a cookie or a bagel or a cinnamon roll the size of your head. Grab a snack and steal a listen before moseying along on your stroll.

Take a right on Elm and walk back to West Cascade. It's time for the "one-two punch" of the most culturally authentic

Sisters destinations, in my opinion. First up is Sisters Market and Eatery, which has ATM and beer signs flashing in the windows and looks like a mini-market. That's because it is a mini-market, but one you'll never forget. I have some friends who got engaged at the Sisters Market. At this Western-fronted, highway mini mart, they laid down their intention to spend their lives together. I thought they were out of their minds until I wandered inside the market myself one day, on a Sisters Folk Festival-timed walking tour just like this one. My husband and I ventured inside innocently enough, our two small children in tow, looking for a cold drink or maybe some goldfish crackers. We didn't leave for at least an hour. Turns out, the Sisters Market is a crazy happy vortex in the center of town, drawing you in and daring you to try to leave.

It went like this. We walked through the doors. One of the first things we saw was some kind of western diorama. It's free standing in the middle of the room, and looks like somebody's old front porch with a bunch of crap hanging off of it, including a fishing creel, a lasso and some horseshoes. If you're like me, it'll take you a really long time to figure out the point of this thing, because, while there is a sign, it's behind an oil lamp and some other stuff. I'll just tell you—the "front porch" is part of the Sisters Market's original storefront, which was built around the turn of the century. But who really even cares what it is—there's an exhibit in a convenience store! I love this stuff. The kids will love it too, although the mannequin people are a little creepy.

But there's more. The grownups, if they are like me anyway, will be equally entranced by the Beer Cave. A molded rock structure with a "Keep Out" sign on a door is guarded by some kind of crazy pirate and an actual bear (albeit stuffed) wearing a straw hat and a red bandana (is it Henry?—see Mitchell chapter).

I realize I am an anomaly in terms of my outsized appreciation for Oregon quirk, but I can't tell you how delighted I was with the whole scene. Add to the porch and the cave the fact that there are a lot of Pacific Northwest microbrews to choose from, complimented by tables, chairs and board games by the windows, inviting mini-market visitors to stay awhile. We grabbed a couple of beers, which the clerk gladly opened for us, and some snacks for the kids, and hung out sipping Oregon craft beer while our children made installation art out of backgammon and checkers pieces. I highly advise this as an entirely valid way to experience Sisters.

What next? Naturally, the only sane thing to do after drinking beer in a mini market in a Western town is to go cowboy boot shopping. You're in luck—there's a Western clothing shop next door to the market, the other half of the Sisters cultural "one-two-punch." Dixie's Western Wear offers a wide selection of authentic cowboy and cowgirl clothes. After that 22-ounce bottle of IPA I consumed in the market those years ago, I came *so* close to buying some cowboy boots in this shop. The only thing that stopped me was the price tag. It's expensive to be a cowboy, apparently. You might be bolder than me, in which case you'll continue this walking tour booted, heeled and fabulous.

From here, you can return to the Village Green Park for more music and romping; check out a few more cool Sisters shops like Canyon Creek Pottery or Eurosports; or go for the full debauchery plan and wind your way into the Sisters Saloon and Ranch Grill. Built as the Hotel Sisters in 1912, this watering hole has anchored the main drag, welcomed newcomers and loosened up the locals for well over a century. The bar is a masterpiece of the elements of an old saloon, including tall bar stools, well-worn floorboards and taxidermy animal heads. There's a restaurant side of things as well, if you have the kids in tow, and in season, you can sit outside. Steaks and burgers are balanced with salads from locally grown produce. All are chased down with the adult beverage of your choice. Welcome to Sisters! And, cheers!

## *Sidetrip*
# WHYCHUS CREEK

If you need a little more nature in your day, or you wish to hike off that pint and burger, visit Whychus Creek north and east of town. The area was the site of the first settlement here: Camp Polk, a military post in the mid-1800s. Today it's the location of some great hikes, a waterfall and plenty of natural beauty. Whychus also has an interesting history of cattle grazing and subsequent restoration that is a great example of a collaborative conservation success story in the American West. Find the trailhead to Whychus Falls off of Three Creek Road south of Sisters: it's a moderate hike along a creek canyon with a view of the two tiers of the falls at the end.

## *Overnighter*
# THE SISTERS BUNKHOUSE

There's a new bunkhouse in town. The Sisters Bunkhouse is located right in downtown Sisters and has four cozy and pleasant rooms for rent. The location is great—nowhere else has such easy access to all of downtown's Western kitschy charm. The rooms are even numbered with horseshoes, though you'll need to bring your own horse.

# SISTERS

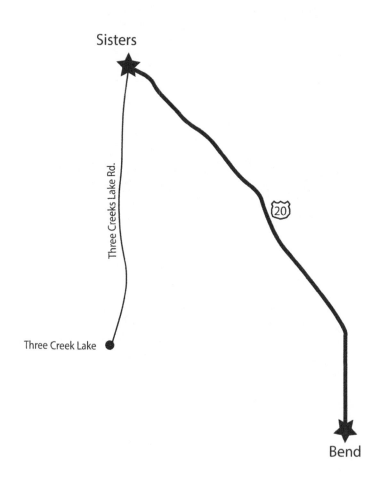

# THREE CREEK LAKE

## Alpine hikes, wildflowers and White Russians

*Distance: Three Creek Lake is 40 miles north and west of Bend.*

The first time I visited Three Creek Lake was also the first time I drank White Russians. I was in college and had tagged along with some friends to the lake for a camping trip. Camping, during that time in our lives, meant pitching a tent next to a lake and drinking. (You know you did it too). Get enough Kahlua and vodka in you and you might even feel like jumping in a very chilly alpine lake (I say from no particular personal experience). Considering that Three Creek Lake is at 6550 feet elevation, its clear waters stay pretty cool, even in August. You jump in; you jump back out. You dry off in the sun. You drink another White Russian. Repeat.

The second time I visited Three Creek Lake was ten years later. I discovered what none of the tipsy, lazy youth on that first trip bothered to discover—if you put down your drink and climb that hill next to the lake and hike across an alpine plateau, you land in the lap of the mountains. It's stunningly beautiful. Keep going and you encounter glaciers, cerulean-blue glacial lakes, rocky basalt pinnacles, stunted forests of subalpine fir and a cliff-top view to knock your socks off.

The third time I visited Three Creek Lake, I was pregnant. No White Russians. Less hiking, more nausea. It was still beautiful.

Which is all to say that there are many ways to enjoy this

gem of a lake in the Cascades. Three Creek Lake is at the base of the Cascade Range, south of Sisters. The lake is also an example of how many different ways there are to get into the Cascades. From Bend, we tend to go up Cascade Lakes Highway, for convenience. Three Creek Lake is on the other side of Broken Top from Cascade Lakes Highway, only accessed by driving northwest from Bend to Sisters and then south, climbing the road to the lake. It's also only accessed by a one-way-in kind of route that's not plowed in the winter. Never mind the out-of-the-way feeling of the place—that's part of what makes it totally worth the trip.

On your way through Sisters, grab some brunch snacks at Angeline's Bakery or the Sisters Bakery, or better yet treat yourself to a gourmet breakfast at The Cottonwood Café. Longtime Jen's Garden fine dining restaurant owners shifted gears to create casually elegant breakfast and lunch fare that is absolutely divine. The benedict or breakfast burrito will fuel you well into the day. Visit Sisters Bakery if you don't mind the line out front and want a gooey bear claw so big it might last you until next Wednesday, and visit Angeline's if you want gluten-free and vegan options as well as homemade granola.

Follow Three Creek Lake Road out of Sisters to the end of the pavement, and continue onto a gravel road to the lake (this is the same route that you take to access Whychus Creek and Falls, in the previous chapter, though you'll take a right at the sign to Whychus off of Three Creek Road on that journey). It's about 16 miles total from Sisters. Three Creek Lake is a cirque, or glacially carved, lake with a shore that varies from beach to gentle slope to rocky cliff, all surrounded by an old growth forest of ponderosa and lodgepole pine.

To recreate the Three Creek Lake journey of my youth, pull out the beach chairs and the cooler of PBR and White Russians and hang out long enough to make The Dude (a la *The Big Lebowski*) proud. Done!

For the reenactment of my second trip, let's take an incredible hike up Tam McArthur Rim. You may not think you know this rim, but in fact you've seen it from Bend many times—it's the long, low ridge that blocks many Cascade Mountain views from town, especially from Awbrey Butte and the westside of Bend.

From Three Creek Lake, however, Tam McArthur is not only pretty in and of itself, but provides access to that high plateau and those killer views I mentioned a minute ago. The trail begins very steeply, with many switchbacks. On the open plateau, it flattens out, and you'll travel a few miles until a final ascent to the cliff-edged viewpoint with views of Broken Top and South and North Sister. In the distance on a clear day, you'll also see long-distance views extending north to Mount Washington, Three Fingered Jack, Mount Jefferson, Mount Hood and Mount Adams in Washington State.

Although the trail officially ends at the cliff overlook, you can choose to continue west along the rim top for some ways, eventually traversing a red cinder cone and ending at Broken Hand—an incredible basalt pinnacle over a small glacial lake. This is the real deal photo op. You've probably seen it already in some marketing photo or another and just never knew where it was. The whole hike is about 10 miles out and back—long but rarely steep. By the way, here's your hike trivia—Lewis "Tam" McArthur worked for the Pacific Power and Light Company and was also the secretary of the Oregon Geographic Board. Here is an example of the pros and cons of being immortalized—be careful what you accomplish, or you might get a view-blocking ridge named after you.

A better hike for little ones or the grandparents in town is Little Three Creek Lake. The trailhead is just before the Driftwood campground on the gravel road on the north end of Three Creek Lake, and the hike is about three miles round trip. It's lovely, flat and with views of Tam McArthur Rim and the smaller Little Three Creek Lake itself.

After your hike, break open your thermos of White Russians. Oh, you didn't bring any? Maybe that's good because your Three Creek tour isn't complete without the eponymous brewery in your future. Sisters' first, and so far only, craft brewery is named—you guessed it—Three Creeks Brewing Company. (The lake is actually named Three Creek, though the colloquial name, and the brewery name, is Three Creeks.)

This large dining destination on the Five Pine campus on the southeast end of Sisters has good beer and even better food. Check out the bar if you're kid-free—it's spacious and casual. The dining room has several options, from large tables to booths, as well as a few overstuffed chairs in front of a fireplace. They've named their beers after local places, animals and western ideas—my favorite is the Hoodoo Voodoo IPA, named after the ski area up the road. I like the Knotty Blonde, too, though the hot cowgirl with the smoking gun on the label doesn't look anything like me, and furthermore I don't think that they mean for the name to refer to tying knots in fishing line, or wood grain.

Head back to Bend, full of alpine lakes, mountain peaks, a little craft brew and a delicious dinner. Or if you're like me, glad you didn't drink any White Russians and/or aren't pregnant.

## *Sidetrip*
# THE GALLIMAUFRY

Like several Sisters institutions, the store the Gallimaufry defies definition. Except for that, in fact, it *is* the definition. What the heck is a gallimaufry? I had to look it up. Turns out it means a confused jumble of things. Suddenly, this store makes perfect sense. In the front is a very diverse collection of touristy, gifty items, from candles to calendars. In the back is a liquor store. The only one in Sisters, in fact. So if you are interested in those White Russians and forgot your own provisions, this is your spot. While you're there, you can also buy a picnic basket, an American flag or a Sisters Quilt Show tee-shirt (your mother will love it).

## *Overnighter*
## FIVE PINE RESORT

Five Pine Resort makes for a great getaway. This campus east of Sisters feels Western like the rest of the town, if Western is pretty luxurious. Visit the spa, catch a movie, hit the Sisters Athletic Club (if you're feeling virtuous), grab a brew at Three Creeks Brewing Co (if you're not). Fall asleep in a romantic luxury cabin with a view through the window of towering ponderosa pines.

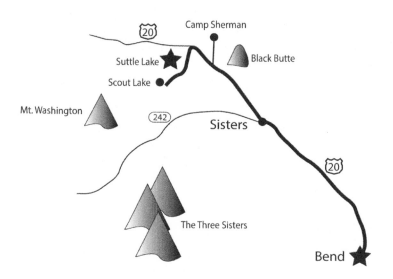

Camp Sherman

20

Black Butte

Suttle Lake

Scout Lake

Mt. Washington

242

Sisters

20

The Three Sisters

Bend

# SUTTLE LAKE

## Clear waters, easy hiking and a retro-cool boathouse

*Directions: Suttle Lake is 36 miles northwest of Bend.*

Sometimes you just need to jump in a lake. Or maybe hike all the way around one, and then jump in it. All of Central Oregon's lakes offer charms, but Suttle Lake stands out as a unique option. Carved from a glacier at the base of the Cascade Range, the long, narrow moraine lake is tucked into the forest at the point where Highway 20 begins its climb over Santiam Pass. This means the lake is easily accessible from the road, while still nestled in an alpine landscape. It's also beautiful, comes with a variety of outdoor recreation, and provides the opportunity for a delicious and somewhat hip lunch at the Suttle Lake Lodge and Boathouse.

This day trip is going to be about hiking, eating and beach lounging—as well as that lake swim, if you're up for it. Grab your hiking boots and your beach gear and head out. Don't forget water and sun protection, and some foods.

As glaciated lakes tend to be, Suttle is shaped like a very elongated egg. The lake is 1.4 miles long and 0.4 miles wide. When travelers climb Highway 20 west towards Santiam Pass, the extended, narrow shape is clearly visible from above, the product of a long-ago glacier carving its way through volcanic substrata.

From Bend, travel west and north through Sisters and continue past the turnoff for Camp Sherman. Suttle Lake is signed with a big Forest Service monolith from the highway, just past the big bend in the road that leads to the climb up to Santiam Pass. Follow signs to Suttle Lake Lodge then keep right to park at the day-use area.

We're going to start our day trip with a hike. A 3.6-mile trail loops Suttle Lake; the trailhead begins at the day-use area. I always find lake loops to be very satisfying—a great way to get some mellow exercise and see the variety the area has to offer without gaining or losing a lot of elevation, and without retracing one's steps.

Lake loops are great for kids, too. My especially children love the Suttle trail—it's flat and fun. They always seem to find fairy houses under trees and shrubs, remember the time that Daddy fell into a nest of bees right after the trail begins and did a little manic dance, journey out to the end of each overlook along the way, and have fun chasing each other along the trail's easy rises and falls. Several years ago, I led my two daughters and my parents around the entire lake—a bit of a feat I wasn't sure would be successful but somehow was and no one even hated me afterwards (though there was some mild complaining throughout).

The first stretch, beginning counterclockwise around the lake, travels below the highway; you'll hear cars and trucks barreling along the road, seemingly overhead. It's pretty and forested through here, with good views across the lake. At the far end of the lake, halfway through your hike, is a dock, a boat ramp, and the first of several campgrounds. It's a good place to grab a drink of water or use the facilities if you need to. From here the trail loops around the end of the lake and travels east past a series of campgrounds. Back at the east end of the lake, the trail travels well into the forest away from the lake to reach the bridge that crosses Lake Creek. Lake Creek is Suttle's only outlet and flows from here four miles to join the Metolius River near Camp Sherman. It's very pretty back here in the woods, and you may even see a few fish, butterflies, or perhaps a deer while you travel through.

After the bridge, the trail trends back towards the lake and to the lodge. Suttle Lake Lodge changed ownership several years ago and is now under the purview of a longtime Portland hospitality business. Though there was some Central Oregon-style ambivalence about the big city folk taking over this old-time lodge, the new owners have made some welcome changes to the property—mainly, at the Boathouse Restaurant. The space sits adjacent to a dock at the edge of the lake and had been closed for a year or two when storm and water damage took its toll. Renovated to offer counter service, with cheerful, white-painted booths, the addition of an old-timey juke box, and with small but delicious meals created with care, the new Boathouse feels like the best of classic woodsy lodge meets fresh new excellence in a clean, simple atmosphere.

Pull up a chair indoors or out, and nosh on a burger or BLT with a view of the lake you just circumnavigated. Once you've let your food settle, head for the beach, back at the day-use area. Some of the lakes of the Cascade Lakes Highway, like Elk Lake, are actually fronted by sections of rocky, jagged a'a lava. That is not the case at Suttle, though the volcanic origins of the lake are still apparent on the beach. Here you'll find a rocky gravel, unlike the course sand found at most of the Cascade Lakes. These little round volcano bits are like marbles, or cobbles, and the kids like digging through them and just plain sitting in them (they are smooth and warm in the sun).

Suttle is a great lake for all kinds of water activities. Bring your various paddling objects, a floaty or even your motorboat, or just pull up a beach chair and chill with your toes in the water while you watch everyone else play.

Another bonus to the southeast beach is that it is the last bank of the lake to absorb the late afternoon sun. I love that feeling of soaking up the day's last rays, watching the shadow of the forest creep across the lake towards you as the sun dips over the trees on the horizon. When the shadow reaches you and the sun drops over the Cascade Range, it's time to go home.

## *Sidetrip*
# SCOUT LAKE

For a smaller, more secluded experience, visit Scout Lake, in the forest behind Suttle Lake. Travel around Suttle and follow signs up the hill, where Scout sits in a deep bowl-shaped indentation in the landscape. This small cup of a lake is removed from the bustle—many people don't even know it exists. Scout Lake holds the heat in its shallow concave waters and windless shores. It's ideal for kids who can wade and paddle in this shallow, safe lake to their heart's content, while parents set up shop on the shore and enjoy a relaxing afternoon.

## *Overnighter*
# SUTTLE LAKE LODGE

The lodge is a blend of rustic and less-so, with nicely appointed rooms in the lodge itself, newer lakeside cabins and rustic cabins to choose from. Inside the lodge, visit the Skip Bar for breakfast, lunch and dinner as well as lovely freshly made cocktails any time of day. The lodge has a huge lakefront lawn with views and yard games like cornhole. Or, use that big ol' lawn to get hitched. Suttle hosts lots of weddings as well as family reunions and the like. There's nothing like the peaceful woods to bring everyone together.

# SUTTLE LAKE

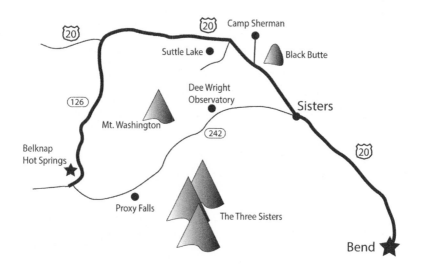

# HIGHWAY 242

## Volcanic vistas, waterfalls and hot springs

*Distance: Belknap Hot Springs, the farthest destination on this day trip, is 70 miles west of Bend.*

Many road trips are about the destination—about getting somewhere. Others are more likely to be about the journey, and about enjoying awesome destinations along the way. The Oregon Scenic Byways program exists to identify the best road trips in the state, the ones that are good for a journey. They might also get you somewhere, but possibly not quickly, and with plenty of scenery and worthy pit stops along the way.

Highway 242, or the Old McKenzie Highway, is one of my favorite Scenic Byways—incredibly pretty with wonderful recreation and sightseeing opportunities. And it's easily accessible from Bend, at least during the summertime (in the winter it isn't accessible at all—the road, like the Cascade Lakes Scenic Byway, is only open seasonally).

Choose a beautiful late spring, summer or early fall day and hit the road! Pack hiking gear, a cooler, layers of clothing and your swimsuit. We're doing it all today. Head north and west on Highway 20, making a stop in Sisters at The Depot Cafe or Oliver Lemon's Market to pick up a picnic lunch. The Depot Café is known for fresh food made from local ingredients in a cozy atmosphere. They are experienced at packing up picnics to go—try the classic egg salad or Greek salad packaged for the road. Oliver Lemon's is a grocery store and more, with gourmet foods, beer and wine, and homemade soups and sandwiches to go. They have some fun gift items too, and you might find yourself walking out the door with a cutting board shaped like Oregon or a paperweight painted with a colorful local landscape.

Picnic tucked away in the cooler, head west out of Sisters past the high school to reach the outset of Highway 242. Casually, 242 is known as the Old McKenzie Highway, which is exactly what it is. It was constructed as a highway in the 1920s, but the route already existed as a wagon trail, established in the 1860s. It was the only highway east over the Cascades from Eugene until Highway 126 was built in the 1960s. Today Highway 242 is nobody's fast way to get over the mountains. Equal parts narrow, winding and indirect, 242 is the exact true nature of a scenic byway. This means you need to carve out a day to experience it when you aren't making a beeline to the Willamette Valley, like we Central Oregonians so often are. The entire length of Highway 242 is less than 37 miles but you should expect to take several hours to make the journey and give proper due to the sights and experiences the road offers. You won't regret it.

Many of the chapters in this book give nod to volcanic activity, and this day trip is no different. The landscape all around us in Central Oregon is volcanic in origin. All of the Cascade Range's peaks are volcanoes, and guess what—they used to erupt. Some will erupt again, but we're not discussing that just now. It scares my children, and anyway, scientists say we'll have plenty of warning, I promise.

Past eruptions left behind many lava flows—the whole region is really one big lava flow. Some lava flows are under dirt and not as obvious. One of the coolest features of Highway 242 is that it takes you near distinct, immense black lava flows. The road passes through miles and miles of lava beds. The chunky black lava contrasts with the white mountain peaks in the near distance and the hopefully-clear-blue sky for some truly awesome sightseeing and photo opportunities.

From Sisters, drive Highway 242 fifteen miles to an amazing place to take all of this in—the Dee Wright Observatory. The observatory was built during the Great Depression by a Civilian Conservation Corps crew that was stationed at Camp Belknap, near Clear Lake. It was completed in 1935 and named for the construction crew's foreman, who had died the previous year. It's an open shelter built from the very volcanic basalt lava rock that surrounds the site, with open-air windows framing the gorgeous Cascade peaks. You're on top of the world here, at the summit of the pass at over 5000 feet, and it affords a panoramic view of the mountains, including Mount Jefferson, Black Butte, Belknap Crater, Mount Washington and Mount Hood. Especially on a clear day, it's stunning. There is also a "peak finder" on the observatory roof to help you identify which mountain is which.

Take a little time to hike the half-mile Lava River Interpretive Trail, which begins at the observatory. It's paved, easy for the kids or grandparents, and offers interpretive signs with more info about the incredible geology all around. (There's a much tougher, but very rewarding, trail called the Obsidian Trail further down the road. You must plan ahead by acquiring a special entry permit to hike this one—it's limited entry for good reasons including incredible views of meadows, mountains and streams as well as obsidian cliffs, once a great source of material for tools made by the Native Americans. It's an 11-mile loop and worth every mile.)

There are a few picnic tables at Dee Wright Observatory, perfect for enjoying the lunch you brought, with a view. As you munch your picnic lunch, consider this—the McKenzie River, which we'll see later in today's journey, originates under all of this rock. The river is fed by a network of vast, cold-water springs that lie under these lava flows; the springs feed nearby Clear Lake, which is the headwaters of the McKenzie (you can learn more about this area in the Upper McKenzie day trip coming up). It's a unique hydrology in that it results in a clear, cold and very consistent water flow year-round. And it all begins under the lava at our feet.

After lunch, we've got some more exploring to do on this historic highway. The road continues, dropping out of the lava flows into a forest of Douglas fir, hemlock and alder. Here the road becomes very winding, following switchbacks through a forest. For this reason, it's a bad road to try to travel with a trailer or other oversized vehicle, or children that are prone to vomiting.

Speaking of vomiting, we interrupt this chapter for a brief personal bathroom story. Once when I was traveling Highway 242 many years ago, I needed a bathroom when there wasn't one to be found. So I jaunted off into the woods. Little did I know I was relieving myself on a nest of yellow jackets, who took advantage of my exposed flesh to sting and sting some more. I think the final count was eight bee stings, some on body parts that, as my daughter says, haven't been discovered yet because they are private. Don't do that. Just hold it.

Towards the end of the switchback-laden section of Highway 242 is a real treat (and the site of a toilet, yay!). Upper Proxy Falls and Lower Proxy Falls are two of the prettiest falls in the state. They are well-signed from the road, and a short loop hike takes you to see these gorgeous cascades. Upper Proxy is one of the most frequently photographed waterfalls in Oregon. Fed by springs on the shoulder of North Sister, Proxy Creek breaks over a wall of columnar basalt covered in plenty of Western Oregon moss, separating into a two-streamed veil that's just beautiful. It's a great, easy hike for the kids and a must-stop on this journey.

From here, it's only another 6.5 miles to the junction of Highway 242 and Highway 126. Next up is what you've been waiting for all day even if you didn't know it—a soak in a hot spring. Take a right and head east just one mile to Belknap Lodge and Hot Springs. Guests can rent a cabin, stay in the lodge or camp here, but the great news is that you can also pay a small fee and soak in the two mineral springs pools without staying on the property. A natural hot springs source feeds the pools (more volcanism at work), which are nice concrete vessels set in spectacular landscaped grounds with a view of the aforementioned spring-fed McKenzie River. The bubbling sounds of the river serve as a soothing backdrop to your warm, rejuvenating soak. Can't beat that!

Soak until you've had your fill, then take a short walk across the footbridge that crosses the McKenzie River to get a glimpse of the famed McKenzie River Trail. Popular with hikers and especially mountain bikers, the 26-mile trail winds through thick, green, western Oregon woods, full of wildflowers, flowering shrubs like rhododendron and serviceberry, and plenty of trees from vine maple to Western red cedar to red alder to Douglas fir. It's worth a short walk along the river—or a long one depending on how energetic you feel. Don't leave without finding Belknap's secret garden.

Some people claim the energy of the volcanoes flows through visitors to lava-laden areas, providing energy and inspiration. Maybe that's how you feel after this day of scenic byway, volcanoes, and hot springs.

Return to Highway 126 and make your way east to Central Oregon by the "fast" route—over the "new" McKenzie Highway: Santiam Pass.

## *Sidetrip*
## BLACK CRATER

Black Crater is a shield volcano accessed off Highway 242. It's a great hike, steep and challenging with killer views. It's seven miles out and back and climbs from shadowy forest to open rocky scree to a giant lava field, which flowed from Little Belknap 1,600 years ago and Belknap Crater 1,700 years ago. The finale is a pinnacle summit with sweeping views of the Cascade Range and surrounding smaller buttes. This one is challenging—don't take the kids or your mom but do enjoy this awesome workout with a great payoff.

## *Overnighter*
# BELKNAP HOT SPRINGS RESORT

Stay at Belknap Hot Springs Resort. It's so pretty here, with the manicured gardens and the lovely, amazing McKenzie running by. You're so relaxed from your soak in the hot springs pool, and wouldn't it be nice to skip the driving home part and just check in to a cozy hotel room or cabin? Just do it. It's only an hour and fifteen-minute drive back to Bend in the morning—you can even make it to work on time if you want. Or not.

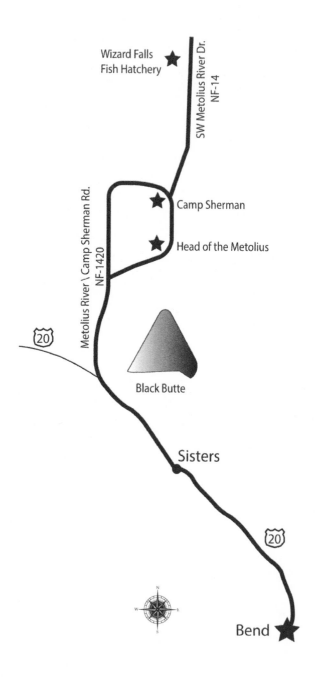

# CAMP SHERMAN

## Fish hatchery, country store and a river that springs from the ground

*Distance: Camp Sherman is 37 miles northwest of Bend.*

Camp Sherman is one of my favorite places on the planet. The small, forested community at the base of Black Butte is only 40 miles northwest of Bend but reliably delivers a peaceful, nature-infused, old-timey getaway. If you're like me and still appreciate visiting places without reliable cell service, you'll like Camp Sherman. This small, charming community provides a rare opportunity to unplug in more ways than one.

Camp Sherman was established in the early 1890s by wheat farmers from Sherman County, looking to escape the summer heat of their grassy fields in north-central Oregon by lounging by the cool waters of the Metolius River. Since those wheat farmers first tacked up a shoebox sign declaring this area as their own summer camp, not too much has changed. This place is home to a few lodgings, a tiny school, a fire station, one restaurant and one store. Two rows of rustic cabins on the banks of the river house a few year-round residents, and more that are part-time.

Camp Sherman is 15 miles northwest of Sisters on Highway 14 off Highway 20. It's a great destination nearly any time of the year—in the spring, it's fresh and lovely, in the fall, the foliage colors are amazing. Summer is, like everywhere else in Oregon, divine. Winter is great too if you're up for cross-country skiing or snowshoeing instead of hiking.

Before you leave home, consider packing a lunch. Camp Sherman's restaurant scene has been a moving target in the last few years, even before COVID-19, but especially since COVID-19. At press time, there was a Peruvian restaurant called Hola! open most days 1 to 8 p.m. Lake Creek Lodge has a restaurant that is open for breakfast, lunch and dinner, sometimes. I wouldn't count on either without calling ahead in advance. Your only other lunch option will be a packed picnic or the Camp Sherman Store—more on that in a bit.

After passing through Sisters, continue past Black Butte and take a right at the Camp Sherman signs. Immediately a forest surrounds you, comprised of incense cedar and lodgepole pine with snowbrush under the towering evergreens. Also almost immediately, your cell service begins to wane in the shadow of the small volcano Black Butte. Though I many times have been the dumbass in Camp Sherman waving my phone over my head trying to get a signal, I advise you to stick the thing in the glove box and forget about it. You'll be much happier later. Continue several miles across the bridge on the Metolius River and then past the aforementioned Camp Sherman Store, following signs to your first stop—the headwaters of the Metolius.

It's not every day that you see a river spring literally from underground, or as it appears, from a rocky, fern-covered hillside in the woods. The Metolius forms from underground springs and appears here, before running its short 29-mile course to terminate at Lake Billy Chinook. The headwaters are conveniently accessed by a short, paved quarter-mile trail that also boasts a direct view of Mt. Jefferson. Depending on the season, you might see many people or none, but chances are you'll encounter a mighty band of yellow-pine chipmunks accustomed to dining on visitors' treats. (The kids will love them.)

As you watch the water trickle from the earth, consider that no one seems quite sure of its source. The presumption is that the source of the Metolius springs is a basin on the other side of Black Butte, and that the eruption of the butte itself is what buried the river's more obvious origin. But when we visited here when my daughters were small, they always insisted that there were fairies in these woods. I like to think perhaps the Metolius is the work of those fairy kingdoms.

After your short hike to the magical beginnings of the Metolius, it's time to go and see some fish. Just as the chipmunks at the headwaters are accustomed to bite-sized handouts, so too are the fish at the Wizard Falls Fish Hatchery, our next stop. Directly north of the headwaters nearly 7 miles, the hatchery's collection of green buildings and holding ponds is the birthplace of six varieties of fish; a total of 2.5 million fingerlings are distributed around the state from this location each year.

Grab your quarters from the car—25 cents buys a fistful of fish food dispensed from vending machines to the kid's hands so that they can toss, sprinkle or hurl it into a long cement pool to the mouths of hundreds of various-sized trout. The rainbow trout, kokanee and salmon raised here always act like they've never been fed before (also like those chipmunks), and will energetically leap and swipe at the scattered bits. It's great entertainment for all ages. At the far end of the hatchery is a large pond holding the biggest fish, as well as offering the best view of larch- and pine-covered Black Butte towering in the distance. There are several picnic tables on the property, too, great for lunch packed from home, if you brought it. If not, our next stop is the Camp Sherman store, your source for mid-day provisions and eats.

The Camp Sherman Store is a classic—an old, log-cabin-like structure stocked with a huge variety of goods from sun-proof clothing to fine wine to canned soup to Klondike bars. It's open year-round and caters to campers, locals, visitors and fly fishermen, and is the only game in town. Therefore, it functions as the heart of the community. Spend some time perusing the place or sitting out front on the log bench sipping a cool drink or devouring an ice cream. The staff will pop open your Pacific

Northwest craft beer or uncork your Oregon wine for you to drink outside. Additionally, you can acquire a full lunch—there are plenty of packaged foods as well as a deli that can produce fresh sandwiches. On hand are also espresso, sodas and the like. A few picnic tables sit under the canopy of vine maple on the north side of the store. Guess what? There's no cell service here, either. Kick back and pretend you don't have a job.

After lunch or a beer, stroll across the street to the overlook and take in the beautiful Metolius. The river is known for being a very challenging fly-fishing river, and you'll likely see a few anglers trying their hand at catching a trout.

Adjacent to the store and bridge is also access to the Metolius River Trail—if you're up for hiking, here's your chance. The trail is extremely pretty, following the gentle, clear river for several miles. You'll pass many small campgrounds that sit along the river—a great opportunity to scope them out for a future stay. Look for Canada geese, mallard ducks, deer and beaver. The trail is flat and easy and therefore good for kids or older family members, and you can turn around and head back whenever you want.

Depending on how far you hike, you may reach the Metolius River Canyon. The trail here climbs out of flatter meadows to a cliff that offers amazing views of the water as it is compressed to travel through a narrow canyon. Look for osprey and hawks as well as deer. Because it's closer to the Cascade Range, the forest in this region of Central Oregon is more diverse than further east in the high desert, and you'll see larch, alder, serviceberry, snowberry, spirea and more along the riverbank. This section is also popular with kayakers, and you may see some boaters winding their way down the cold narrow waters of this river.

Return the way you came and end your Camp Sherman day by dipping your toes in the river. Maybe grab one more snack or sip from the store. Think about those wheat farmers and how smart they were to choose this place. Then drive back out to Highway 20 and head for home.

Fine, you can have your phone now, but for gosh sakes, pull

over to answer all those texts and emails you missed while you were relaxing and having fun instead.

## *Sidetrip*
# BLACK BUTTE

Nearby Black Butte is a terrific, classic Central Oregon hike. The butte is 6400 feet in elevation, but because the road reaches halfway up the butte, the summit is reached with only a 1600-foot-elevation climb. It's a steep but relatively short hike, and in under two miles you'll reach incredible views of the Cascade Range, Black Butte Ranch and Suttle Lake. There is a great mountain finder on top to help you identify what you see, and there are also a couple of historic fire lookouts, too. When I stay in Camp Sherman for several days, I always try to fit this hike in. Makes a lazy afternoon with a beer by the river even more satisfying after you've climbed an extinct volcano.

## *Overnighter*
# LAKE CREEK LODGE

Camp Sherman is most definitely a day trip so enchanting you might just want to stay. A great lodging is Lake Creek Lodge, a family-favorite getaway location that has been in existence in one form or another since some of those early days of the wheat farmers. The first lodge was built in 1924 on the banks of the meandering, lovely Lake Creek. My family and I have overnighted at Lake Creek Lodge many summer nights, sleeping soundly despite the yips of a pack of excitable coyotes howling at the moon. Come dawn, we awake to cool mountain-air mornings, the sweet smells of ponderosa pine and snowbrush, and pink sunrises promising sunny days. Magical!

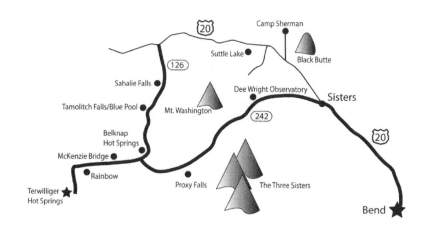

# UPPER MCKENZIE

## Mountain biking, lush forests and peaceful getaways

*Distance: Rainbow, the farthest destination on this day trip, is 80 miles west of Bend.*

Living in Central Oregon means being blessed with many dry and sunny days. The sun shines here; the rain, mostly, does not fall, and this is typically a very good thing. But that aridity also defines our landscape, or, as many call it, our monoscape. We have ponderosa pine and juniper here, sagebrush and manzanita—all of which are mostly monochromatic shades of dark and sage green. The sun we like, but the grey vistas on every horizon can get tiresome.

Our quickest green fix is the McKenzie River. It's only just over an hour's drive from the west of Bend to reach its headwaters; from there are many options for outdoor play. In the earlier chapter on Highway 242, we discussed the scenic byway that leads to the McKenzie, and the river's volcanic origins. In this chapter, we're going straight to a day of play on the river itself.

Eat a big breakfast, pack some snacks, or grab some food in Sisters—it's likely you won't find services on the McKenzie until later in our day trip. Pack hiking shoes and clothes and layers of clothing, including a raincoat. The McKenzie area is a million shades of awesome green for a reason, and that reason is water, which often falls from the sky as rain.

Travel over Santiam Pass, continuing west on Highway 20 until canting south at the Highway 126 fork. Clear Lake is your first stop, only a few miles from the junction. We're going to begin our McKenzie exploration with a hike around the lake. It's 4.6 miles, flat, and an excellent overview of the McKenzie ecosystems, which include lava fields, spring-fed waters, and those gorgeous green forests. The trail passes through all these landscape variations in its loop.

Clear Lake is long and narrow; the front side is the Clear Lake Trail and the backside is the famous McKenzie River Trail. This latter trail is what most people know about the McKenzie River—it is 26 miles of incredible beauty mainly known as a very challenging mountain biking trail. (More on that a little later in this day trip.)

Park at the Clear Lake Resort, where cabins, camping, rental boats and a small weekend-only restaurant are available. Begin your hike from here, clockwise. As you hike, remember that Clear Lake is the headwaters of the McKenzie River. Let's recap the hydrology of the McKenzie. Above here, in the lava fields of the Cascade Range, a vast network of cold-water springs feed Clear Lake, which then feeds the river. The lake was formed by a lava flow 3000 years ago, which created a natural dam, which backed up water into a lake. The water leaves Clear Lake at its western end to create the McKenzie River.

Because it is spring fed, the McKenzie maintains a constant water flow year-round, which is good for fish and boating enthusiasts. It also means the water is stunningly, beautifully clear, and cold, cold, cold. You can swim at Clear Lake, but you might not want to.

After your hike, back in your car, travel a mile or so south to the turnout to Sahalie Falls. This is one of the prettiest, most accessible falls in the state—easy parking off the highway allows for a short hike to an overlook with great views of this wide, crashing falls, named after a Chinook Indian word for sky or heaven. There's so much water here, from the river, the waterfall spray and the rain, that the forest is dense and amazing.

This is your first real taste of the lushness of the McKenzie — compared with the grey-green of Central Oregon, everything here looks neon. It's almost stimulus overload to step into this forest from the car. The layered forest of hemlock and Douglas fir is stunning. There are dozens of species of trees, shrubs, and wildflowers, including vine maple, alder, serviceberry, wild rose, trillium and red flowering current. Because this place is so very accessible, it gets a lot of visitors. Please respect signs for parking and stay on designated trails. The wild green landscape is not invincible, and hundreds of footsteps a day can do great damage to the beauty and resiliency of this beautiful spot. If Sahalie is full, continue down the highway to another destination, some suggestions for which are up next.

From Sahalie, hike downstream on the Waterfall Loop Trail to Koosah Falls, just a mile away. Here the river throws itself off another cliff to majestic result. (The terrain here is the result of a series of lava flows over the last 3000 years, creating the aforementioned dam at Clear Lake, these falls and the large section of basalt that forces the river underground below here). From a lower, railed vantage point, on the right day, the sun streams through the trees and hits the water spray of Koosah just right to reveal an incredible rainbow. We stood and took that in for a good while. The green of the forest, white of the river, mist of the spray and colors of the rainbow combine to make just about the world's perfect photo opp.

You can continue downstream and make a loop of this hike by cutting past Watson Reservoir to connect with and loop back on the McKenzie River Trail. Follow the road once you reach Watson, staying right, and you'll see signs for the trail tucked off the side of the road. Alternately, return the way you came to Koosah. If you've used up all your juice hiking around Clear Lake, it is also possible to skip the hike altogether and visit Koosah by way of car, via the Ice Cap Campground entrance, and a very short hike.

The trails you've been walking are classic "McKenzie" — presenting with some lava flow, some dense tree root systems, some staired climbs, some narrow and rocky passages. I mentioned earlier that the McKenzie River Trail is considered a mountain bike classic in the American West. But as you've hiked over this rugged terrain, you may have wondered who in their right mind bikes here. The trail can be tough going even on foot, and I've heard just as many people say biking here is overrated and difficult to the point of being un-fun as I have heard say it's utterly awesome and epic. You say tomato, I say to-mah-toe. Anyway, I wouldn't bike it. But you already knew that, because I have been perfectly honest with you all about my un-super-rad existence. I'm just reminding you that you don't have to be a badass to live in Bend, even if it sometimes seems that way.

Next up is another hike. One of the most incredible spots on the McKenzie is the Tamolitch Pool. Unreachable by car, the Blue Pool must be hiked or biked to, making it even more mythical and worth the payoff. The trail begins at the upper end of Trailbridge Reservoir. Look for signs to the reservoir and then to the trailhead. The trail travels two miles upstream to reach Tamolitch Pool. Remember how I mentioned earlier that the river dives entirely under a lava flow for a stretch? That happens between Koosah Falls and here; Tamolitch Pool is where the McKenzie reemerges from underground. It's an incredible, round concave of blue water bigger than it looks in photos and quite amazing.

The first time I hiked to Tamolitch, I was pregnant. The last time I hiked it was ten years after that and somehow it felt more difficult than when I had a baby inside of me. Ah, aging. Such a joy. The trail isn't a big deal but can seem rugged and long. It can be quite busy too, as so many people have discovered this magical place in recent years. The trail climbs from a fir forest to high cliffs with amazing views of the river. There is minimal elevation gain on this hike, but it is very rocky in places, passing through the last of that lava flow that covered the river. In this section, we saw a lot of people with bicycles who weren't riding them, but instead tugging them along over jagged lava rock, making me glad I had only my mildly aching feet and not a bike to deal with. Just about when you're sure you've somehow missed it, the pool appears before you—serene and lovely. There are several places around the rim to sit and rest your feet or get crazy-brave and scramble down the sides to reach the water, which, like everywhere else on the McKenzie, is cold cold cold—try 37 degrees in the summer.

By now you're starving and, after you hike from the Blue Pool back out the way you came, it's time to beeline for civilization and food. Oregon has grown so much, and is such a tourist destination, that finding good food these days isn't that difficult in much of the state. But there are times when you'll feel the rural state of this place, and the whims and risks of the open road, and this is one of those. Belknap Hot Springs (also discussed in the Highway 242 chapter of this book) is the first place you'll reach as you continue to travel west on Highway 126, and while a soak is a great idea, it'll be a hungry one—at last notice their restaurant was closed (though in recent history there was a food cart stationed on site in summer, offering burgers and the like).

McKenzie Bridge is five miles from there, towards Eugene, and there you'll find a general store as well as a place called McKenzie Station Pub and Espresso. It looks promising, if eclectic, with way too much of all kinds of décor going on. We stopped there on our last visit. Inside, we found everything from old paperback books to memorabilia of The Beatles to stained glass lamps to keychains for sale. I was charmed by the homey, quirky feel until we realized the service was absolutely terrible and that we would be stuck there for the better part of eternity waiting for a meal. Luckily, maybe, our McKenzie Station Pub tenure coincided with the only torrential downpour we saw that day, which we enjoyed through the windows rather than on a trail. It was also a good reminder that the weather on the McKenzie is finicky—it can go from sunny to rainstorm to sunny in 20 minutes. Still, by the time we were finally allowed to pay our bill and leave the McKenzie Station

Pub and Espresso, I would have gladly hiked back to Tamolitch in a monsoon rather than stay there another minute.

So don't eat there. Where should you eat? Try Takoda's. It's another five miles down the road and has been around for a long time, reliably serving pizza and burgers with casual indoor and lovely outdoor patio seating. There's also a new-ish spot called the Obsidian Grill, located in the courtyard of the McKenzie General Store in McKenzie Bridge, that gets pretty good reviews.

You've earned your meal with all that hiking, so make it a generous one. Then find a little riverfront spot to rest up. Despite the never-ending gorgeous natural beauty, it can still be difficult to locate a little piece of hang-out riverfront on the McKenzie. There's a lot of private land and super-forested riverbank. Try several of the campgrounds that have day-use areas, with restrooms and tables. They are perfect for setting up for a picnic or to splash in that river (did I mention that it's cold?). Try Ice Cap, Paradise or McKenzie Bridge Campground Day Use areas.

When you've had enough, journey back on Highway 126 for home, watching the landscape get greyer and simpler, but knowing that your next McKenzie Day Trip is always just around the corner.

## Sidetrip
# TERWILLIGER HOT SPRINGS

When I was a college student at University of Oregon, Terwilliger Hot Springs was a legendary place that I heard a lot about but never visited. Creepy, fantastic, dangerous, party-central, beautiful, littered and magical were just some of the words I heard about the place. Since then, some of the litter and danger have been cleared out. It's still clothing optional, and it's still a place you might prefer to visit in the relatively safe, and sober, light of day, but if you're adventuresome you might just want to see these five, partially developed pools of natural hot water off Highway 19 (Aufderheide Highway) south of Rainbow. There is a day-use fee of $6, and a short hike to reach the pools.

## *Overnighter*
## EAGLE ROCK LODGE

A bit further downstream from McKenzie Bridge is Eagle Rock Lodge in Nimrod. My husband and I discovered this place when friends were having a camping birthday party nearby and we didn't want to camp. Eagle Rock turned out to be a true pleasure. This old lodge is located on a gorgeous bend in the river, with a huge lawn and rocky beach to hang out on. The lodge serves a delicious breakfast on an expansive deck also overlooking the river. Rooms were quiet and comfortable. I'd go again in a heartbeat.

# NORTH

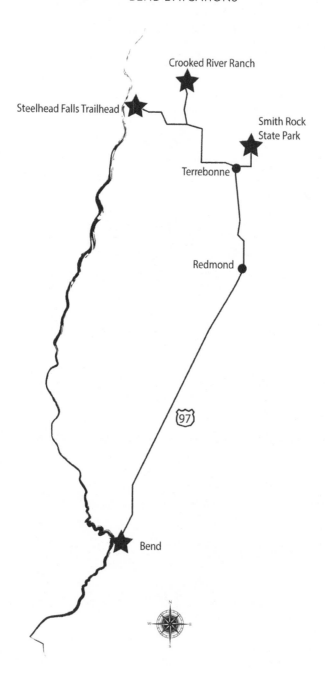

Crooked River Ranch

Steelhead Falls Trailhead

Smith Rock
State Park

Terrebonne

Redmond

97

Bend

# SMITH ROCK

## Serene spires, rail cars and buffalo nachos

*Distance: Smith Rock is located near Terrebonne, 25 miles north of Bend.*

I have a friend who chose the top of Smith Rock as the place where he would first try psychedelic mushrooms. He and some college buddies climbed to the top of Misery Ridge, ate the shrooms and frolicked around under the influence for what he described as a very long, colorful and spiritually amazing day.

Don't worry—I am not going to use this book to advocate for the best places to take drugs in Central Oregon. Quite the opposite, unless the "tripping" part of day tripping with children or your visiting parents feels to you like being under the influence (which it might). I relate the story of my young friend because, although I thought he was out of his mind in more ways than one (it's a long way to fall from the top of Smith Rock), I understood his location selection. Without drugs, I've always found Smith Rock to be a mindblower. The incredible orange-blue-grey spires that reach to the sky contrast with the blue sky and the Cascade Range in the distance all make this place unlike anything else you've seen—it is at once quintessential high desert Oregon and a magical destination that could be on the moon. But it's more than just the scenery— Smith does feel spiritual. It's hard for me to visit Smith and not feel a little opened up inside, newly reminded of how incredible and beautiful our world is, and each of us is totally insignificant yet utterly alive. I've never taken psychedelic mushrooms, but maybe the experience is a little bit like that.

Aside from spiritual enlightenment, Smith Rock is a terrific day trip in many other ways. It's close to home but just far enough to feel like you've gotten away, super easy to access and weirdly almost always basked in good weather. The climate here tends to be a little bit warmer and drier than elsewhere in Central Oregon, and the rocky spires further serve as collectors of that additional heat. The rock soaks up the sun and then reflects heat back on the earth and Smith Rock's visitors. Year-round, it's likely to feel hotter here—in the summer you may wish it didn't feel so hot, but in the winter it just might be balmy enough for a hike, even if it's snowing in town.

A note: the myriad charms of Smith Rock, and its easy access, have not gone unnoticed by the masses. Smith Rock has gotten a lot of attention since Travel Oregon named it one of the 7 Wonders of Oregon in a marketing campaign several years ago, and visitor numbers have risen dramatically. Smith is very, very busy these days. I strongly suggest choosing an off-season or mid-week time to visit the spires. Please respect signs regarding trail closures and the like. Dogs must always be leashed, and please pack out their poop. Speaking of poop, there are restrooms near the parking lot but not a lot of potty options once you head down into the canyon, so plan ahead.

Okay, public service messages completed—let's get this day trip started. Smith Rock is located east of Terrebonne, which is 24 miles north of Bend on Highway 97. Start your day by grabbing some provisions on your way north. There are no concessions or services at the state park (though, when the Rockhard store, en route to the state park, is open, don't miss the chance to try their phenomenal ice cream). There are several markets and restaurants in Terrebonne, such as Ferguson's Market and Oliver Lemon's, so you could grab something there. Or, depending on where you are leaving from in Bend, stop at Sparrow Bakery in NorthWest Crossing for a latte and an ocean roll (an amazing cinnamon-roll-like treat made with cardamom) or a bacon breakfast sandwich, or Nancy P's Bakery for a savory pocket made with bacon, egg and cheese or a yogurt parfait. Alternately, stop in Redmond at Honey and Pine Coffee or Proust Coffee, both in downtown, for a latte and baked good.

As you enter Terrebonne look for signs directing you to turn right on Wilcox Avenue. Follow signs to Smith Rock State Park, winding past agricultural parcels and a few homes to the parking area. Parking can be tight here, especially on a weekend, and requires a state park pass or a $5 voucher available at a kiosk in the lot. The parking area sits on a rim above the Crooked River canyon. From here, begin your visit by walking paved trails and gazing across open spaces at Smith Rock's awesomeness and the snow-capped peaks of the Cascade Range in the distance. It's an accessible, jaw-dropping scene and photo opportunity from the parking lot alone. This vantage is up close enough to be a thousand times better than spying Smith Rock from Highway 97 while zooming by at 65 miles per hour (though there are worse views from highways).

But to really get the full Smith Rock experience, hike down a steep, dirt and gravel hill to the Crooked River, cross a bridge and put yourself at the base of the rock. From here, you can make one of three trail choices: proceed straight forward up the steep climb to Misery Ridge; take a right and travel upstream to see lesser-visited Monument and the Gorge areas; or take a left and travel downstream for an easy hike that will allow views of many rock climbers and lead to the one, must-see iconic park attraction, The Monkey Face. It's a 350-foot-high monolith with a top that, from the right angle, resembles a monkey's face.

I recommend the latter. It's the easiest option, following a river trail journey that is two and a half miles out and back to the base of the Monkey Face spire, friendly to hikers for its flatness. (This is a great one for the kids, and I've taken my girls on this trail many times). It's very safe, while still offering the occasional boulder on which the kids can practice their rock scrambling skills. As you wind around the base of Smith Rock, you'll take in its beauty from many angles. Keep your eyes peeled for wildlife in and around the river—I've seen otters, birds of prey, fish and rattlesnakes (for the reason of the presence of Oregon's most famous venomous reptile, don't reach your hand into dark rocky crevices here, or send the kids into rugged, shady passageways unless you're fond of trips to the ER or calls to poison control).

As you hike, you'll see rock climbers galore. While locally loved for its beauty, Smith is famous around the globe as a rock-climbing destination. Climbers from places near and far venture here to take advantage of the several thousand established climbing routes. When you reach Monkey Face, gaze upwards and see if you can spot some brave souls clinging to the rock.

The other trail option, to Monkey Face, is for those looking for a good workout. From the bridge at the base of the trail from the parking lot, continue straight ahead and up the hill along the Misery Ridge Trail. It's aptly named—only two-thirds of a mile but steep, the climb offers a killer payoff: views of the Cascade Range, Smith Rock itself, the Crooked River and the Oregon high desert. It's exposed and not a great choice for young kids (or those who hate exposure and/or hiking uphill), but it's incredible when you reach the top of the world, Smith-style.

At the summit of the Misery Ridge Trail, you'll also reach an upper-level view of Monkey Face: from the area called the Spring Board at the top of the trail, you'll be looking straight into the monkey's mouth. You might see climbers perched in the monkey's mouth who have climbed from the base. Some daredevils even string ropes from the ridge into the mouth and tightrope across. It makes my stomach clench to even think about it, but it's pretty awesome to watch.

While you're hiking, contemplate the geology of this place. It's long been known that Smith is comprised of welded tuff from volcanic ash cloud deposits. But only in the past two decades has it been discovered that Smith Rock is the northernmost rim of the Crooked River Caldera, a gigantic 420-square-mile caldera tens of millions of years old. Gaze closer at the rocky cliffs around you and see where the dark, 400-foot-tall spires of rhyolite (a more viscous, slower-flowing lava than basalt) cast upwards through the lighter, bleached faces of welded tuff. The pyroclastic ash cloud created during the collapse of the great caldera deposited the tuff. The rimrock cliffs you see across the river to the south are much more recent—basalt flows from Newberry Volcano 1.2 million years ago.

Aside from spring and fall hikes, one don't-miss time to visit the Smith Rock area is in October, when a few local farms open to the public as pumpkin patches. While these events have become more commercialized, crowded and expensive in recent years, they are still a rite of passage every family should undergo. Visit DD Ranch, where the kids can take a hayride, pet farm animals and play on a menagerie of rope swings, slides and hay mazes, as well as, of course, acquire a pumpkin to take home. It's positively gorgeous out here in October, and the light is divine for family photos. DD may also be selling their organic grass-fed beef, frozen so it'll survive the drive home, as well as local honey. They also sometimes sell burgers and beer, usually welcome treats to kids and adults (respectively). Another great destination is Smith Rock Ranch, home of the Maize. Each year a themed maze is carved through acres of corn, inviting guests to enter and try to find their way to the center, and then back out again. (Don't worry, there's a map). Smith Rock Ranch also has a pumpkin cannon, pony rides and a zoo train.

A trip to Smith is never complete for me without a post-hike lunch stop at Terrebonne Depot. This restaurant, in an old train depot, serves delicious homemade foods. I like the nachos with buffalo meat, but the ahi tacos are also amazing. If you thought you couldn't get fresh, lightly seared ahi in the high desert, you will be pleasantly surprised. Terrebonne Depot has a great kid's menu and homemade desserts too. Regional craft brews and cocktails too? Check.

Sit outside if you can—the deck has a view of Smith Rock and sits just feet from the railroad tracks. Trains still pass by several times a day, unleashing tremendous energy and bringing up a breeze as the cars fly by in a whirl of color. That, plus an Oregon microbrew or fresh mixed cocktail, will round out your spiritual input for the day, sending you on your journey back home invigorated and satisfied, with no psychedelic mushrooms required.

## *Sidetrip*
## DESCHUTES RIVER TRAILS

Approximately five miles to the northwest of Terrebonne in the Crooked River Ranch housing development are 10 miles of trails with incredible views of the Deschutes River, the Cascade Range and Smith Rock, and hardly anyone knows about them. The trails travel rimrock ridges, allowing hikers to peer into the canyon below or at the majestic mountains in the distance. You can access these trails at three trailheads. To reach the Otter Bench trail, turn into Crooked River Ranch and continue past the golf course to the end of the road by the river, about 11 miles from Highway 97. Look for a trailhead sign and map. Parking is free. River Road leads to Steelhead Falls, a 20-foot high, river-wide waterfall on the federal wild and scenic middle section of the river. Look for raptors and spring wildflowers, and, in the summer, swimmers and cliff jumpers splashing in the water. Meadow Road leads to the Scout Camp Trailhead, which drops to the river with a descent of 700 feet right across from the place where Whychus Creek enters the Deschutes. In all three cases, it's beautiful here.

## *Overnighter*
## CROOKED RIVER RANCH

There are a few cabins for rent in Crooked River Ranch, only 10 minutes from Smith Rock State Park. The Crooked River

Ranch Cabins allow you to stay out in the high desert instead of returning to the bustle of town, with the smell of sage, the brightness of stars and maybe even the howl of coyotes keeping you company through the night. The cabins give great access to the above-mentioned trails, as well as provide a grassy area on-site for the kids to play. This is a very simple, peaceful place to stay, with incredible sunsets.

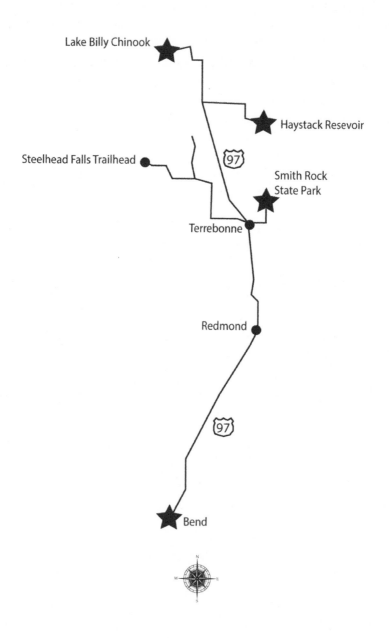

# HAYSTACK RESERVOIR AND LAKE BILLY CHINOOK

## Motorboats, rimrock views and rivers colliding

*Distance: Lake Billy Chinook, the farthest destination in this day trip, is 44 miles north of Bend.*

It isn't every day that three rivers collide, especially in a dramatic rimrock high desert canyon. The result is one of Oregon's most distinctive lakes and a scenic and recreational paradise, Lake Billy Chinook. We'll get there, but first on this day trip we're going to check out a classic high desert reservoir.

Oregon has many reservoirs, and it's worth mentioning that their true purpose isn't to satisfy our desires to play in nature. No, reservoirs weren't created for fishing or boating or camping, but to hold water in reserve for use in irrigation, mainly. Nevertheless, most reservoirs are open to the public for recreation, and lucky for us, we actually do get to fish and boat and camp at these watery oases. Haystack Reservoir, created in 1950, is one of these places.

I had never been to Haystack Reservoir until a few years ago, despite easy access off of Highway 97 north of Terrebonne. From Bend, travel 45 minutes north to a right turn, to the east, that is well-signed. Travel through a landscape of sage and juniper for just a few miles to the lake. Haystack Reservoir is within the Crooked River National Grassland, which consists of land reclaimed from abandoned homesteads. These lands were typically used (farmed or grazed) beyond what they could easily recover from (in terms of water use or soil depletion), which often resulted in damaged ground cover. Haystack Reservoir is a great visual example of the high desert landscape, and of an ecosystem that has been heavily used by cattle in the past.

There is a day-use area on the east side of the lake. We were there on Memorial Day, and there was hardly a soul in sight. This is one reason to go to Haystack; though it's true that the day-use area is nothing fancy, you'll have some space to yourself, which isn't always the case in Central Oregon these days. The lakefront is muddy and grassy, and the lake water green with algae, but there are picnic tables to be had and entertainment to be found. There are lots of birds here—we saw eagles and vultures and many other smaller birds. Our kids entertained themselves by skipping rocks for an hour. We saw some fish jump. What else do you need?

Maybe some scenery. Another reason to go to Haystack—perhaps the primary reason—is the view. From the day-use area, skim your eyes over the small lake along a beautiful copper-colored rimrock outcropping to a perfect view of Mt. Jefferson in the distance. The mountain is just amazing from this angle—a perfectly sloped, snow-topped shape centered in your view to the west.

When you've had your fill, continue your day trip by heading west from Haystack, crossing Highway 97 and dropping into Culver. The little farming town of Culver has more going on than you might think. With 1300 people, a couple of burger joints, a market and such, this little town sustains its own. In the summer, Culver blossoms as the gateway to Lake Billy Chinook. Locals rent boats, water gear, and sell lots of sandwiches and fuel to folks coming to enjoy the local lake. This was welcome news for us when we rolled into town with a nearly empty gas tank. Culver has gas and diesel! Yay.

So, back to that three-rivers-colliding thing I mentioned. The

Deschutes, the Crooked and the Metolius River meet here. It is the Round Butte Dam that manifests their confluences into a lake, and a most interesting one at that. Because of the deep canyons here, each river has backed up into a long skinny arm of lake. The arms are surrounded by steep canyon walls and are each equally fun to explore. For reasons of steep walls and deep water, Lake Billy Chinook is best known for boating, especially house boating and ski boating. The large, beautiful, three-armed lake is deep and striking, and great for fishing, waterskiing and just generally speeding around. But here's the good news—you don't need a boat to enjoy the lake. There is hiking, sightseeing and lakefront play to be had here, as well, boat-free.

A note for the curious—the Crooked and Metolius Rivers terminate at Lake Billy Chinook. It is the Deschutes River that continues north out of the reservoir, beyond Round Butte Dam and then Pelton Dam, further downstream, making its way another 100 miles through the high desert, at which point it merges with the mighty Columbia.

Back to exploring Lake Billy Chinook—from Culver, the road cuts in descent over a steep canyon wall. You'll immediately see the expanse of the lake as you drive down the angled grade, as well as the rimrock walls of the canyon. The geology here dates back to about 11 million years ago, when the volcanic Cascades began delivering basaltic lava, stream sediment and volcanic debris to the landscape. Then, just one to three million years ago, lava flows capped the land with the striated, striking rimrock we see now. Over time, the rivers did their handiwork to carve canyons through all of these layers of stone, as they continue to do today.

As you reach the lakefront, stay left, pass Crooked River Day Use Area, and follow the road around the canyon. Not far from the day-use area, you'll suddenly come across a beautiful waterfall, informally called Billy Chinook Falls, which tumbles over the steep rimrock wall at the side of the road. It's surprising the way the tall falls just appear from on high. The water is mostly irrigation runoff, so the flow will vary depending on the time of year. There's not much of anywhere to pull over so give it a good gawk as you drive (safely) past.

Continue on, across a bridge hanging over the Crooked River arm of the lake and pass through a narrow saddle between the Crooked and Deschutes river-arms. The peninsula on your right here is called The Island. It is surrounded on three sides by vertical cliffs 200-feet high. There is a trail at this end, but you can't hike up there anymore, unless you are an educational institution or conservation group. Still, as you drive through the saddle, gaze upwards at the flat rimrock formation and consider this: Because of isolation and steep cliffs, The Island has never been grazed by livestock (unlike almost all of the land in the entirety of the high desert plains). This means The Island shelters one of the last remaining undisturbed examples of two ecosystem communities: western juniper/big sagebrush/ bluebunch wheatgrass, and western juniper/big sagebrush/ bitterbrush. Some people get very excited about this sort of thing—and with good reason as so much of the West has been trampled and altered by us human folk. Oh—there's also an unusual lizard community up there on The Island. Once upon a time, a striped whiptail lizard apparently escaped from a recreational vehicle and got to work making a family on The Island. Tell the kids that—they'll have swarms of lizards dancing in their heads at least long enough to keep them distracted until you get to the next day-use area.

Continue past the Deschutes Campground to the Lower Deschutes Day Use Area. It's a short hike downhill from the parking lot to the water, where you'll find a lovely place to hang out, partially shaded by many trees including pine, juniper, poplar and Russian olive. There are bathrooms, picnic tables and a swimming area enclosed by a floating barrier to keep boat wake from disturbing the water too much. The kids will love walking the barrier and swimming. When we were there, we had left the swimsuits in the car, and no one wanted to hike back up the hill, so the kids just jumped in with their clothes on. Why not? It's summer in Central Oregon. And clothes dry.

As you kick back with a cold beverage (don't forget to schlep that from the car), you might wonder who this Billy guy is. Billy Chinook was a Native American of the Wasco tribe who traveled alongside American explorers John C. Frémont and Kit Carson as a guide in their expeditions of 1843 and 1844. His gravestone, in the Warm Springs Reservation, reads: *A faithful and true friend of the white man.* Little did he know that legacy would get him a gigantic three-armed reservoir named in his honor. And so it goes with the human quest for immortality— you never quite know how it's going to work out. (Incidentally, "Culver" was the first postman in town, who named the city after himself. That's one way to play the immortality game.)

From this day-use area, or from the Deschutes Campground nearby, you can access a trail similar to the one that is closed on The Island. The Tam-a-lau climbs 600 feet in elevation to reach the top of the high plateau called The Peninsula. Spectacular views of the Cascade Mountains and the Crooked and Deschutes River canyons, as well as of The Island, are yours for the taking on this seven-mile loop.

When you've tired of lakefront play or hiking, drive back the way you came (gawk at Billy Chinook Falls again) to the Cove Palisades Resort. Here you can get the best in summertime café fare—burgers, milkshakes, riblets and Cove Chili—to eat outside on the deck, with the lake before you and those amazing cliffs towering overhead. It's the perfect end to your Billy Chinook day as you drive out of the canyon named for an Indian guide in which three rivers collide and across the high desert plains for home.

## *Sidetrip*
## BALANCING ROCKS

There is a truly astonishing piece of geology to be seen overlooking the Metolius River at Lake Billy Chinook. It was my father who led me there for the first time, revealing nothing of our intended destination until we hiked over a hill to suddenly encounter a scene that hardly seemed real. Known only as Balancing Rocks, this place is exactly as the name suggests. A field of massive boulders, each balanced atop a stone spire, are perched on a slope overlooking the Metolius River. The geology goes like this—three distinctly welded volcanic tuffs settled upon one another over time, and then weathered away at different rates. The top layer essentially protected the erosion of the bottom layer—now the protector balances precariously on that which it protected. At 13.7 miles west of the Deschutes River arm bridge, look for the balancing rocks parking area and trailhead 0.1 mile west of the junction with Forest Road #1170.

## *Overnighter*
# BLACK BUTTE RANCH

From Balancing Rocks, take Forest Service Road 11 west around the back way, ending up in Camp Sherman. You can stay at my favorite lodging, Lake Creek Lodge, or continue on to Highway 20 and then southeast to Black Butte Ranch. Check out their modern and beautiful restaurant space, the Lakeside Bistro, and rent a luxurious two-story townhome on Phalarope Lake. Then kick back in front of the large picture windows to take in truly stunning sunsets and sunrises over the meadow, the lake and the Cascade Range. Far better than a houseboat, in my opinion.

HAYSTACK RESERVOIR AND LAKE BILLY CHINOOK

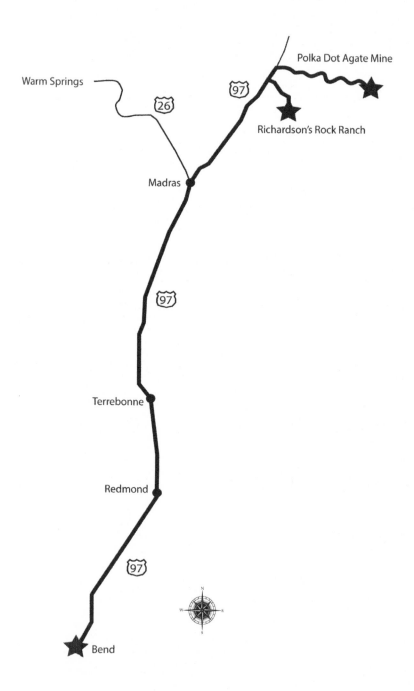

# MADRAS

## Thundereggs, waterparks and alpacas

*Polka Dot Agate Mine, the farthest destination in this chapter, is 67 miles north of Bend.*

Visitors come to Bend for many reasons, but one local tourism booster you may not have considered is rocks. Each year, tens of thousands of people from all over the world visit Central Oregon, also known as the rockhounding capital of the world. All this time that you've been gazing at mountain peaks and flowing rivers, you didn't know that right under your feet was a sea of stony treasure? Well, now you do. Strap on your boots, because today we're marching out into the high desert in search of some darn fine rocks.

First, let's delve into a natural history lesson. A volcanic storyline pops up repeatedly in this book, for our entire landscape is built of the work of volcanoes. Black a'a lava flows, cinder cones and rimrock cliffs are the most visible volcanic creations. But from time to time, Central Oregon's volcanoes formed specimens even more amazing, and a little bit harder to find.

Agate, quartz and jasper were formed in the earth after volcanic eruptions 40 to 50 million years ago laid down rhyolite lava flows, and then cracks in the lava filled with silica-rich water that manifested into these valued rocks. More recent volcanic activity created obsidian (made when lava cools very quickly), like that in the Newberry Crater's 1300-year-old Big

Obsidian Flow discussed in a later chapter.

But the piece de resistance of rock varietals around these parts is the thunderegg. Rightly so, as Central Oregon has the largest thunderegg deposits on the planet. The thunderegg is so renowned that it was named Oregon's state rock in 1965, after regional rockhounds voted it so. Oregon's state rock it remains, though it's true that many people still have no idea what a thunderegg is.

There is some speculation about how thundereggs were formed, but it likely went something like this. The orb-shaped treasures were also formed in rhyolite lava flows by way of silica-rich water, but in the case of thundereggs, the water-filled gas pockets instead of cracks in the lava, therefore forming a round object (hence, the use of the word "egg").

Thundereggs vary in size, and generally are about the size of a small orange. The exterior matrix material of a thunderegg is dull and lumpy, but the inner core is comprised of agate or chalcedony, often shot through with beautiful colors created by minerals. Thundereggs might even have a hollow center, containing beautiful deposits and patterns and even crystals. Each is unique. This is why a thunderegg search is an exciting, mysterious treasure hunt—until you crack one open, you have no idea what is inside.

There are several places to find thundereggs in Central Oregon. A simple Google search will reveal destinations but be aware of the legality of collection on specific lands if you set out on your own. Here, I'm going to make it easy for you—today we're headed to two places that are a guaranteed mother lode of thunderegg excitement: Richardson Rock Ranch and Polka Dot Agate Mine north of Madras.

Before you set out, pack good shoes, clothing appropriate for the weather, and sun protection—rockhounding is a business that exposes one to the elements. We'll be in the desert: bring water and snacks. Bring gloves, a small hammer or pickaxe if you have one, and a bucket. Also know that the ranch is open year-round, but the mine is only open for digging seasonally, usually beginning in May and extending through November, Wednesday through Saturday.

Head north on Highway 97 past Terrebonne and Madras, and then travel another 11 miles north on 97. Along the way, stop to pick up a picnic lunch and use the bathroom—the ranch and mine do not cater in food service or restroom facilities. Turn right at milepost 81 and follow signs three miles to Richardson Rock Ranch. The gravel road travels through a wide-open sagebrush expanse with glimpses of rimrock in the distance, hinting at the beauty of the high desert mine to come.

Richardson Rock Ranch sits on the Priday Agate Beds. Priday was a cattle rancher who discovered the beds and opened them up to public digging in the 1920s. In the 1970s, the Richardsons purchased the Priday beds, several other rock beds, and a cattle ranch, eventually deciding to reallocate their attention from the business of cattle to that of Oregon's famous rocks and sharing them with visitors. For decades, the ranch was open for personal digging, but the Richardsons closed their land to the public right around the pandemic, and today, just the store at Richardson Rock Ranch is open to the public as an amazing shopping experience for visitors and rockhounds.

My girls and I rolled into the ranch headquarters on a cool day in late March under a sky full of puffy clouds threatening rain. Before the Richardson rocks could catch anyone's attention, the resident peacocks did. Several of the brightly colored birds roam around the old ranch buildings, perching on various antiquated farm implements and just begging to be photographed. The 12-year-old chased them, Iphone in hand, taking lots of photos.

Peacocks are impressive, but so are rocks. The Richardson store at the ranch headquarters is open year-round. It's not just Oregon rocks for sale here—dozens of varieties of polished and unpolished stones from all around the globe are on display. Rocks are sold by the pound, and rock lovers can choose from mookaite jasper from Australia, labradorite from Madagascar, lavender quartz and more. There are hundreds of geodes imported from all over the planet. (Thundereggs and geodes are not synonymous; geode is a simpler term, meaning any rock with a hollow in it, sometimes containing a crystal. Thundereggs are a specific structure). The store sells Oregon thundereggs, of course, for those who aren't interested in setting out to seek their own treasure.

Stroll through the glittering, colorful piles of rocks outside and then peruse the fancier specimens inside, which are polished and finished and include fine jewelry and desktop trinkets galore. Buy what you like before getting back in the car and continuing to the Polka Dot Mine to try your hand at digging yourself.

Journey back to Highway 97 and drive north less than a mile to take a right on NE Pony Butte Road. Follow signs nine miles to Polka Dot Mine, which also sits on the Priday Agate Beds. There is no cost to visit or to dig but taking what you find home with you will require a fee.

Upon arrival, expect a staff person on hand to give you the lowdown, delivering the how-tos and rules of rockhounding in the straightforward, slightly aggravated manner of someone who says the same thing over and over all day, and who has witnessed visitors do dumb and dangerous things on this land. These directions are thorough and distinct. For example: do not dig into a cliff wall unless your intent is to dislodge rocks from above that might possibly fall on your head. Do not break the rocks just for the sake of breaking the rocks. Do not break your neck, and if you do, it's your own fault. Listen dutifully, borrow digging tools and a bucket should they be available, and set forth on your adventure.

There are several digging beds on the property; they vary in digging difficulty and potential finds and aren't all always open for digging. Make your selection based on what is open, how hard you want to work, and what you hope to unearth.

We arrived at a small parking area overlooking a gravelly hill and a shallow ravine, in which many others eager diggers were already hard at work when we arrived. It takes a bit of scrambling to climb into the ravine and find a spot to start digging. Right away the girls found plenty of lumpy round rocks, holding them out one after the other for me to inspect.

Suddenly, we had questions. What were thundereggs supposed to look like, exactly? Were these globes the exact ones we were searching for? We really didn't know, and there was no one around to ask except other novices. Therefore, we did what all intrepid explorers do—we winged it. Over the course of an hour, we inspected and banged on and shook and threw a whole bunch of rocks in our bucket. Then before we wrapped up our search, we threw a whole bunch of rocks out of the bucket, because you must pay for whatever you bring out by weight, and we clearly had way too much.

I let the girls do most of the digging while I took photos. Our angled picks rang on the rocks like bells, creating a collective cacophony throughout the digging area. The landscape is very austere and stunning on the mine. We were treated to a few raindrops, but nevertheless the wide-open skies and grey-green expanse of the high desert reliably delivered a solid dose of peace.

After the digging, it was time to return to the shop for the great revealing. Our helper took our thundereggs in back to slice them open, returning shortly carrying a perforated tray of half-rounds. The insides of the thundereggs we'd selected were remarkably similar, their centers filled with white and green and dark grey agate. Only one had a hollow center, which was lined with bright white crystals. I felt a little disappointed— had we known more, maybe we would've been able to choose a more diverse collection. But we were assured that you really can't tell what will be inside until you slice them open, and furthermore, ours was a normal "catch"—about 90% of the thundereggs on this property are agate-filled, with crystals being the more unusual find.

Haul your treasures away in your car and return to Highway 97 to head south. But on the way back to Bend, we have a couple more spots to check out. What better counterpoint to objects manifested from Oregon's volcanism than antique aeroplanes and live pack animals from Peru?

The Erickson Aircraft Collection is in the business park on the north end of Madras. Started by Jack Erickson in 1983, the vintage aircraft collection features over twenty rare aircraft, most of which are still in flying condition. Stop by to see classics including the P-38 Lightning, P-51 Mustang, Ki43 Hayabusa, F4U Corsair, SBD Dauntless, Grumman Duck and B-17 Flying Fortress. Admission is $9 for adults. In August, the museum hosts the Airshow of the Cascades, when you can see some of these rare birds in flight.

Next up, alpacas! On the south end of Terrebonne is the alpaca farm Crescent Moon Ranch, where the animals are raised for breeding and their fiber. Alpacas have been bred predominantly in Peru for hundreds of years. In Terrebonne, baby alpaca birthing season just happens to fall during many of the same months as thunderegg digging season (roughly March until September).

If you're lucky, your stop at Crescent Moon will include a sighting of some baby alpacas. Often, ranch owners let visitors walk amongst the newborn animals, called cria. Alpacas are mild-tempered and gregarious, known for demonstrating unique personality traits. See if you can match an animal to each of your family members in temperament before you climb back in the car with your thundereggs and head for home.

## *Sidetrip*
## MARAGAS WINERY

In 1999, Doug and Gina Maragas did something no one thought was possible—they established a winery in the dry and arid high desert. Today, their vineyards north of Terrebonne are a destination for music, wine tasting, art viewing and special dinner events. Maragas Winery grows grapes and makes tempranillo, red zinfandel and more on gorgeous acreage right on Highway 97. Stop by on your way home to sip a taste or two of wine and grab a bottle to take home. Hours vary seasonally; check the website.

## *Overnighter*
# SCP HOTEL REDMOND

Downtown Redmond has experienced a real renaissance in the last decade. The main city blocks always had great architecture but had suffered from setbacks and neglect along the way. An anchor property to downtown rejuvenation efforts that came along in 2018 is the SCP Hotel Redmond. Simple and elegant in design, the hotel has 49 rooms and suites, a market, and a restaurant (vegan food only). The lobby is expansive and includes a massive stone fireplace and comfortable hangout spots. The hotel's crown jewel is on top—The Rooftop bar, where a menu of locally-inspired small plates, handcrafted cocktails and panoramic views of the Cascade Range are on hand. Book a room for a Redmond staycation and kick back for the night.

# EAST

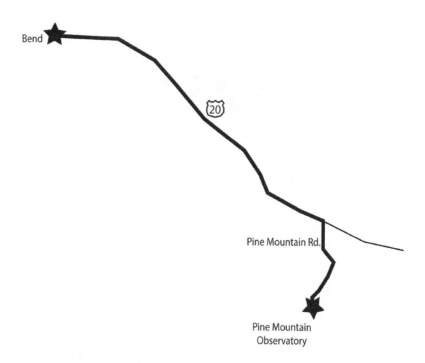

Bend

20

Pine Mountain Rd.

Pine Mountain
Observatory

# PINE MOUNTAIN

## Stars, skies and a stagecoach stop

*Distance: Brothers, the farthest destination in this road trip, is 42 miles east of Bend.*

My first visit to Pine Mountain Observatory didn't go so well. As a lover of romantic nights under the stars and expansive Oregon desert skies, I'd been meaning to visit the observatory east of Bend for a long time. The research facility on top of Pine Mountain is run by the University of Oregon, has several telescopes, is staffed by volunteer interpreters during the summer and was rumored to be great for nighttime stargazing and study.

But the year we decided to go, we waited until the last weekend of the season. We also decided to camp. Turns out temperatures get cold in a campground at the top of a 6300-foot-high mountain in early October. My husband lit a campfire to warm us up and promptly got scolded by the campground host. The season was closed for burning. The weather, however, hadn't stopped the hunters. We'd also timed our visit to coincide with the opening weekend for deer hunting, and the campground was overrun with guns, beers, carcasses and large, noisy trucks/RVs/generators prone to very early and very late hours of operation.

We tried to overcome all of this. Central Oregon is a diverse place, and hunters, scientists and dreamers have long coexisted on these lands. And, after all, we were there to check out the observatory, and that experience was still available to us. But, as these things go, the campground host who had berated us was also the observatory program host for the evening. He had not forgotten us and gave us the stink eye as soon as we entered the large tent that serves as interpretive headquarters. After that inauspicious start, our two young daughters fell asleep during the long and un-stimulating lecture that precedes the use of the telescopes, prompting us to carry them back to the camp and their sleeping bags. My husband stayed there with them, which meant only I returned to experience the famous, expensive university telescopes.

I have to say, I didn't feel my family had missed much. Peering through a telescope in the freezing cold at some blurry far away object reminded me of how I felt when I had taken astronomy in college. The romance of a night sky full of glinting stars that drew me to the subject is not the same as studying the physics of a supernova in a windowless classroom auditorium with 250 other students. One is magic, the other math.

That night, I peered through a few telescopes, taking in the complicated explanation provided to me of what obscure sky object I was seeing. After a while, I stepped back away from the group and gazed at the night sky in the manner I had first fallen for—alone and with no technology assist. Then, though the observatory volunteer was planning to stay out until 2 a.m. to catch some other very important star that was to eventually appear, I drifted into the darkness away from the group, picked my way back through the dark and starry night to the campground, and crawled into the pop-up trailer with my family.

You might think this story was meant to dissuade you from visiting Pine Mountain, but au contraire. Despite being nonplussed by my observatory experience, I still recommend the trip in the right circumstances. It's the classic example of not every day trip being the right day trip for everybody, every time. Pine Mountain is a great choice when you want to pull a science-oriented all-nighter with some friends. Leave the kids at home. Unless they are super science geek kids, and older, they are just going to get bored and tired. Don't go during hunting season, unless, of course, you are hunting. Don't camp—save that for a more scenic destination. Take provisions, add in a visit to an awesome diner for dinner, stay until really late, and then plan on going back to Bend.

Okay, now that we have all of that sorted out, let's start our day (night) trip itinerary. Pine Mountain Observatory is located 34 miles east and south of Bend, perched atop a mountain at an elevation of 6300 feet. The turn is just past Millican and is well marked. But before you climb the mountain, I begin your evening of stargazing with dinner in the desert. Continue east past Pine Mountain to the tiny town of Brothers, 16 miles past Millican on Highway 20. It's small. Blink-and-you'll-miss-it small. But it is home to the Brothers Stage Stop. This destination has been here 100 years and was originally just what it is called, a stagecoach stop between Burns and Prineville. Today it still operates as a restaurant, market, small store and post office, run by a pair of sisters in Brothers.

The Stage Stop is an Oregon classic, a reliable place for American food and a fun place to hang out. It's small, funky and friendly. You never know who you might see in this place—it receives customers from road cyclists touring the entirety of Highway 20, which runs east all the way to Boston, Massachusetts, to hunters passing through, to locals just looking for a great home-cooked meal with friendly service. Sisters Dixie and Jerrie know a lot about this part of Oregon and are happy to share their knowledge. Check their hours online as they vary (they are never open late). At press time, the Brothers Stage Stop was for sale, so make sure they are still open (it would be tragic if they weren't after over 100 years!).

Another amazing thing about Brothers is totally free and inescapable—the view of the Three Sisters Mountains in the Cascade Range. Once you've driven east to Brothers, stop and turn around to look back to the west. The mountains are centered in your western view from the highway and are utterly spectacular. If you happen to hit it at sunset, all the better—

though driving west into the setting sun is hard on the eyes.

You won't have to drive into the sunset for long. Full of delicious dinner, return west on Highway 20 to the left turn up Pine Mountain. From the highway, it's eight miles to the summit, the campground and the observatory. As you climb the 6300-foot peak, you'll be awarded with terrific views of the sagebrush desert below, as well as the Three Sisters and additional Cascade peaks. You can really see the terrain of the high desert from here—Paulina Peak and Newberry Crater to the west, the Ochocos to the north and many volcanic cinder cones sprinkled around to the south. In addition to stargazing, Pine Mountain is known for parasailing. Imagine gliding down from the summit to the desert below, with such scenic beauty around you. That sounds terrifying to me, but to each his own.

At the top, you'll see the telescopes in their domed protective houses, looking like space-age robots planted in the sage landscape atop the mountain. University of Oregon chose the location in 1967, to make good use of the dark skies of this lightly populated section of the high desert for astronomy education and research. Today, interpretive programs only run Friday and Saturday nights in summer (between Memorial Day and the end of September), and are also dependent on weather, moon phase, sunset time and global pandemics (the place was shut tight all of 2020 and some of 2021). Clouds will cancel a program, a full moon will diminish star visibility and a later sunset time will push the program start time back. How late the observatory stays open is up to the volunteer and may be anytime between 11 p.m. and dawn.

If you get to the top well before the tour starts and daylight is still on your side, take a hike. The peak of Pine Mountain is two miles from the observatory, mostly along an old road. It's steep and pretty. Even if you only make it a bit of the way, you'll be treated to terrific views west of the Cascade Mountains and the high desert.

Then, enjoy the show! Don't piss off the interpreter, see

what cool factoids you can glean from the lecture and peer through those high-tech academic telescopes millions of miles into space. Then step away from the crowd on top of this mountain in the desert, turn your face towards the stars and think about magic.

## *Sidetrip*
# THE OREGON BADLANDS

You'll pass the Oregon Badlands on your way to and from Pine Mountain. This nearly 30000-acre wilderness area protects ancient lava formations and juniper trees. The Badlands is a great opportunity to get off of the highway and actually see the high desert landscape. The desert is remarkably beautiful, peaceful and interesting once you get out in it. The Flatiron Trailhead is easy to find; it's right on Highway 20 at the green 16-mile marker. From here you can follow either the Flatiron Trail or the Ancient Juniper Trail for a taste of the desert. You'll be amazed how lovely the juniper trees are up close. Some of these trees are several hundred years old, and as they age they become more twisted and distinctive. The lava rock here is also distinctive—rugged rimrock in rust and dark brown colors. The Badlands are more fragile than they look (hence partly why they've been designated wilderness) so please follow directives on signs, stay on the trail and leave no trace.

## *Overnighter*

I'm at a loss here. My husband suggests parking your fifth wheeler in Millican. I think he's kidding, though.

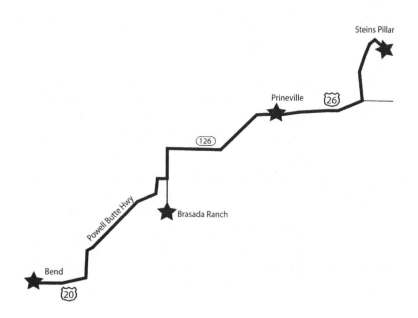

# PRINEVILLE

## Rodeos, Ochocos and history

*Distance: Prineville is 36 miles northeast of Bend.*

Prineville gets a bad rap. The small-town east of Redmond is picturesque, charming and laden with history, yet still has the Central Oregon reputation of being a bit backwoods. Back in the 1990s when I first moved to Bend, one Halloween, I dressed as the Prineville prom queen. I wore an iridescent blue prom dress, fishnet stockings, blue eye shadow and logging boots. I'm sorry, Prineville. The truth is, I'd never even been to your fair city. Maybe passed through once or twice, but certainly had not given it a fair shake. Certainly not enough to think I could fairly dress like your youth.

It wasn't until a decade later that I got out of my car and gave Prineville a chance. What I found made me smile—good people, western history, interesting architecture and a beautiful landscape. The day trip I took there with a friend began in the charming city square, ended with a pint of beer in a legitimate dive bar and resulted in the purchase of my favorite hat.

Prineville is 35 miles north and east of Bend. The most scenic route is via the Powell Butte Highway—itself a beautiful journey and a route I look forward to driving for the views and open space. Head east of Bend on Highway 20 and then north on Powell Butte Road to Highway 126. You'll pass the small but active Bend Airport, as well as many ranches and homes tucked into the sagebrush.

It's easy to forget sometimes that Bend is a vibrant oasis in a vast high desert, and this highway gives a real sense of all that surrounds our fair city. The grey-green of sagebrush and rabbitbrush east of town stretches as far as the eye can see, punctuated by volcanic rimrock in rusty brown shades and the occasional purple or yellow wildflower. Old, gnarled juniper trees are everywhere. Expansive blue sky extends overhead and the Cascade Range from Mt. Bachelor to Mt. Hood is fully visible to the west. It's so pretty here that you should pull over to the side of the road to take a better look. This is an especially good idea because some locals tend to drive this road like their tailgate is on fire. Apparently if you live out here or travel the Powell Butte Highway frequently, you aren't interested in the views, and instead are focused on getting wherever you are going as fast as humanly possible.

After you pull over and gawk, onward to Prineville! The highway descends a steep grade into town, traveling around a big bend carved into the rimrock hillside. Mid-way down, don't miss the turn to the Prineville Overlook, also known as the Ochoco Wayside Point. From here, you can see the Crooked River, the town of Prineville centered in the river's small valley and the Ochoco Mountains in the distance. This is your first glimpse of the town's architectural beauty, mainly the Crook County Courthouse. The clock tower of this fine building rises above the rest of downtown and is visible from the grade and viewpoint.

As you descend the road from the lookout to the courthouse, think about Prineville's history. Prineville is the oldest city in Central Oregon, founded in 1877. Entrepreneur Barney Prine came to town in 1868 and set up shop selling blacksmithing services, dry goods and whiskey. The town flourished until its fate changed drastically in the early 1900s. James Hill and Edward Harriman were two railroad magnates furiously competing to establish a line up the Deschutes Canyon into Central Oregon. They were working their way south from The Dalles, laying track furiously on opposite sides of the river, fighting one another, and dictating the future for a series of Oregon towns in the process.

Prineville was Central Oregon's largest town at the time, and Harriman's enterprise was laying tracks along the east banks of the Deschutes, bound for Prineville. But when Harriman suddenly died, Hill's team won the longstanding rivalry; their tracks to Central Oregon would follow the west banks of the Deschutes, ultimately routing the railroad through the six-year-old town of Bend. The job was completed in 1911, and the rest is history.

This decision left its mark on Prineville and its residents' feelings about Bend pretty much from then on. Still, the city of Prineville came up with their own money to build a railroad connector to the main line, and thanks to the lovely, large and extremely valuable ponderosa pine trees that grew in the Ochoco forests to the east of town, Prineville continued to thrive for many decades. However, as was the case with so many Oregon small towns, when the lumber ran out, the good times quit their joyful gallop and slowed to a very lazy saunter.

Still, Prineville today has a population of over 9000 people and has benefited from Central Oregon's overall growth. There are a few new things in town, but the area has retained its historic charm, and your visit today will be about seeing history and longstanding locals' favorites.

Start your on-foot tour of downtown on the square across from city hall and the courthouse. Here you will find a large and imposing bronze statue of a cowboy on a horse, chasing another bronze horse. Prineville is a cowboy town and not afraid to make this statement right in the center of town. The kids will love checking these guys out and posing for a photo.

Next, venture across the street to the courthouse. Built in 1909, the stately three-story building of stone and brick that you spied from the overlook is topped with a two-story clock tower extending to the sky. It's worth a step inside for its beautiful old architecture, including lofty windows overlooking main street, classic linoleum floors that will remind you of your grade school, and tall wooden office doors with inset glass panels.

There are several parks in downtown Prineville, adding to the charm. Several are along the Crooked River or Ochoco Creek, which also runs through town. Take the kids to run wild and free in the grass at Stryker Park or Pioneer Park before your next stop, the Bowman Museum.

The Bowman Museum resides in an enormous brick building built in 1910 that used to be a bank; today its modern use is as a museum documenting Prineville and Crook County history. Inside you'll find exhibits chronicling the stories of everyone from Native Americans to homesteaders; farmers to ranchers to loggers; and of course the story of Les Schwab, whose entrepreneurial spirit brought tire shops to the entire Northwest, beginning with his purchase of a rubber franchise in Prineville in 1952. Les Schwab Tires was headquartered here for several decades, serving as another of the town's economy anchors.

After your museum immersion, it's time for lunch. Central Oregon's world-famous and booming craft brew scene has extended out of Bend, so don't miss a chance to grab a pint at Crooked River Brewing. Crooked River Brewing brews their own beers as well as offers tap handles pouring other Northwest favorites. The food here is pub style, including lots of pizzas, nachos and sliders.

After lunch, continue your wander through downtown. My favorite shop is Prineville Men's Wear. Even the ladies will love taking a look at this wonderful little Western wear store that seems like it hasn't changed a bit since 1950, when it was founded. Collared shirts with pearl buttons, authentic and awesome cowboy boots, trucker hats galore, belt buckles, bolo ties and more are neatly arranged on crowded shelves and racks and just begging for perusal. There are most definitely women's clothes here, too. I say, buy someone a Christmas or birthday gift here. This store is the source of my favorite hat—a beauty of an oversized ball cap in white and red that reads, not surprisingly, "Prineville Men's Wear."

Another great destination is Good Bike Shop, an excellent

stop for bikes, gear and plentiful local advice on all things biking, from road cycling to mountain biking to gravel road riding to overnight touring. One more place to sightsee, err, shop, is Urban Girl Western Purses (read that name again). Here you can buy Western handbags in sizes tiny to humongous, in themes from Americana to bling. Their specialty is purses that are meant to carry a concealed weapon. You don't see that every day, proving Prineville really is a bit of a throwback to the Wild West.

Another piece of evidence to that theory is the Crooked River Roundup Rodeo and Horse Races. This event in late June is when Prineville comes alive—if you want a true taste of wild, rodeo-oriented good times, plan your visit then. The town is packed with cowboys, cowboy boots, rodeo queens, western hats and probably a gun-toting western purse or two. Drink macro beer, watch bucking bulls in action and bet on a horse race at this event.

Whether you are here for the rodeo or not, don't leave town without a taste of a local watering hole. The truth is, the last time I was in Prineville we meant to go to the Bowman Museum. We were on our way there, in fact, but then accidentally got distracted by the Horseshoe Tavern. This downtown bar has a huge red horseshoe sign hanging out front, which enticed us to make an entrance. Once inside, the classic Americana bar décor, jukebox, pool tables, friendly and colorful bartenders, and awesome people watching entrapped us until past museum closing time. This was the point at which I knew that Prineville had cast its spell on me.

If this happens to you, too, don't fight it. Do as we did, and wander over to Barney Prine's Steakhouse for dinner, where huge portions of excellent food like stuffed mushrooms, ranch-style beans, Texas tri-tip, whiskey chicken or Barney's one pound blacksmith shop steak round out your Prineville day perfectly. Bend can wait—you've got steak and potatoes to put in your belly. When you do finally waddle out the door, don't forget your hat.

## *Sidetrip*
# STEINS PILLAR

Not far past Prineville is Steins Pillar. This amazing geological find is accessed via Mill Creek Road, north of Prineville Reservoir. The pillar is a 350-foot monolith of welded tuff, deposited during the collapse of the Wildcat Caldera around 40 million years ago. The pillar can be seen from the road, but for a better look, hike the Steins Pillar Trail. It's a couple of miles to the base of the pillar, through old-growth forests of ponderosa pine, mountain meadows full of wildflowers and past rocky ridges. The monolith is named after Major Enoch Steen, who explored this area in the 1860s. He's the same Steen of Steens Mountain east of here, it's just that people had a hard time spelling his unusual name. Take Mill Creek Road from Highway 126 and watch for signage that will lead you onto a forest service road to the trailhead.

## *Overnighter*
# BRASADA RANCH

One of my favorite lodgings in the state lies in a place you might never expect. Between Bend and Prineville is Brasada Ranch. This resort is on the flanks of Powell Butte on a property that used to be a working cattle ranch. Today it is an awesome overnight destination, with luxury cabins, two excellent restaurants, a tough and rewarding golf course and the best sunsets in the state. The view is of the vast high desert and the peaks of the Cascade Range in the distance. Try that view out from the amazing pool—which has three hot tubs, a lazy river and a water slide—with a cocktail in hand. At night, the stars are bright, unpolluted by the lights of the city, and the air is cool and smells of sage. It's a peaceful, satisfying getaway, even for one night.

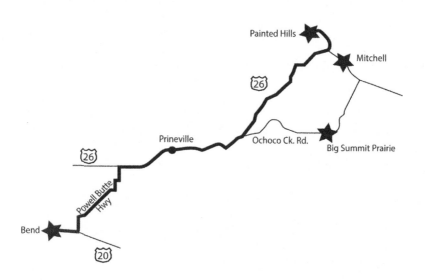

# MITCHELL AND THE PAINTED HILLS

## Layers of ash, great desserts and a bear in a cage

*Distance: Mitchell is 82 miles northeast of Bend.*

There used to be a bear named Henry who lived at a gas station in Mitchell, Oregon. He lived in a big cage, was friendly, liked cookies and provided many travelers with a reason to stop in this very small town east of Prineville. Henry isn't there anymore. I heard that, like many of us, as he aged, he got grumpier. Luckily there are several great reasons to visit Mitchell besides a live bear, including an amazing natural wonder and excellent homemade pie and pastries.

Mitchell is 82 miles north and east of Bend, via Highway 126 to Prineville and then Highway 26 to Mitchell. It's a beautiful drive to get there. The journey takes you into the Ochoco Mountains, through a beautiful old-growth ponderosa pine forest and alongside clear mountain streams and lush meadows riddled with wildflowers and corn lily. Just on the backside of the range is Mitchell.

Here, you'll begin to see glimpses of the geology this region is known for. You are entering the John Day Fossil Beds National Monument at its southwest corner. An impressive rock formation, the Mitchell Rock, looms above the town's entrance. Two cone-shaped hills, Black Butte and White Butte, rise in the near distance, giving a glimpse of what's to come.

The monument is comprised of three distinct geographical areas, designated Sheep Rock, Painted Hills and Clarno, protecting incredible geological features. The Painted Hills—a truly amazing sight to behold—is right near Mitchell and on the agenda for our day trip today.

Mitchell has a population of around 130 people—less than you might encounter in a Bend restaurant on a Friday night. That's another great reason to visit this very small town, in my opinion. I love to get away from the bustle of the city and take in the broad sky and open space without competing with piles of other eager visitors. Still, the scarcity of people means that the entirety of Mitchell's services include three restaurants, an espresso stand, a general store, a gas station and three different types of lodging accommodations. And even this is more than there used to be. A decade ago, the Oregon tourism commission, Travel Oregon, established a marketing campaign titled the 7 Wonders of Oregon. The Painted Hills were identified as one of them, and just like at another "wonder" Smith Rock, tourism to this rural area increased significantly. Now, travelers come here from all over the world. A few years back, I was invited to visit the hills with a group of Buddhist monks from Tibet. You can see a photo of them in their striking red robes with the Painted Hills behind them on my website.

Despite an increase in traffic, given the remoteness of the destination, visitation to the Painted Hills is still modest. You shouldn't have any trouble carving out a little room for yourself here. Bring some food and water and a hat and sunscreen, as it's exposed and dry here, and we won't find food until later in the day.

Travel Oregon may have done a lot to put the place on the international radar, but the Painted Hills were always a primary draw to Mitchell, even before white settlers dreamed up a town called Mitchell and before Henry the bear took up residence at a local gas station. This territory was originally home to the Sahaptin people, who hunted, fished and celebrated these lands; later, in the 1860s, a missionary named Thomas Condon happened through and recognized the importance of the region's many fossils, and those artifacts have been objects of intense study ever since. His work was the precursor to the eventual designation of the federally protected John Day Fossil Beds National Monument. The late 1800s are also when gold was discovered in the John Day region, and Mitchell sprung up as an outpost on Oregon roads leading east to gold country.

You'll reach the turn to the Painted Hills before you reach Mitchell—the junction is a few miles west of town. From the turn, the hills are about seven miles north up Bridge Creek Road. You'll pass through a desert creek canyon, with low grassy hills and not much of a creek. The road carves through these gentle knolls to emerge rather dramatically adjacent to the Painted Hills, where you'll suddenly understand what all the hoopla is about.

The Painted Hills are a geological formation so beautiful that it's difficult to give them justice in words. Gentle mounds of red, pink, bronze, tan and black ash and clay are layered in uneven stripes, surreal and lunar in appearance. This area was once a river flood plain—a lush forest with a warm tropical climate that was home to prehistoric horses, oreodonts, camels and saber-tooth tigers. Over time, layers of sediment of varying colors collected to form these beautiful hills, like the flowing water was laying down a painting to last for all time.

Changes in the weather alter the appearance of the hills. The best time to be here is just after a rain, when the amazing varieties of colors really pop. Snow can also be incredibly dramatic, and in spring, small yellow wildflowers paint their own line drawings on these beautiful mounds of earth. In any season, the hills contrast with the wide-open Eastern Oregon sky, which is often clear blue and dotted with white cotton-ball clouds.

Drive to the main overlook trailhead, which is a great place to start as it allows you to take in the entire incredible scene from a bird's-eye view vantage point. As always, please respect the landscape and park and walk in designated areas. This trail is your primary photo opportunity, and it's awesome. Take some photos, and then stay awhile. The Painted Hills are like other places of almost impossible unearthly beauty that, despite magnificence, can inspire a drive-by kind of visit. Visitors say "oo" and "ah" and "wow" and "I can't believe I've never been here," and take a few pictures, get back in their car and leave. I encourage you to linger. Do the "oo" and "ah," and then hold still. Let the energy of the place start to seep in. Feel how the wind begins to clear out the other noise you brought with you. See how the kids react to so much open space and sky and natural visual splendor.

I'd done the drive-by approach here more than once before I let the place really sink in. My holding-still visit was on that trip with the monks. Watching them wander slowly around, doing nothing in particular but simply being there, made me do the same, and I saw things I might not have. How stark it is. How blinding the sky. How really crazy surreal it is that these hills exist at all. How quiet it is. At the end of their visit, the monks chanted and rang bells and blessed the hills. I drove home in a contented daze.

We can't all visit the Painted Hills with monks, of course. But I think small children can be like little monks. If you've brought some with you, let them show you what is here. Maybe it's a flower, maybe it's a rock, maybe it's a bird on the horizon, maybe it's that they want to set up camp and never leave. It'll be something, I promise.

Before you go, drive on from the overlook to the Painted Cove Trail. The boardwalk through this smaller collection of hills is an easy, short walk, great for those monk-kids or older companions, and offering an up-close look at the mounds. At close range, the hills appear to be comprised of small rocks more than ash, piled into neat, smooth cones of varying sizes, mostly in a rusty, Mars-red.

After exploring and photographing to your heart's content, it's time to return to Highway 26 and take a trip into fabulous downtown Mitchell. I hope you're hungry for lunch. Eating in rural America can feel like a bit of a risk, but over the years I've nurtured a somewhat closeted passion for the diners of Eastern Oregon. There's something particularly satisfying about finding a great little eating establishment in the middle of the high desert. For me, traveling this part of the state is about taking in incredible outdoor vistas between visits to authentic down-home diners.

Your destination is the Sidewalk Café in Mitchell. I sometimes dream about their homemade pie. The same goes for the bacon cheeseburger. You'll leave, as an old friend used to say, feeling "fat, dumb and happy." Go for it here. "No regrets," I always say, especially in Eastern Oregon diner-land, where the calories come with wide-open skies and plenty of outdoor activities to burn them off. Still hungry? Need a snack for the road? There is an amazing bakery called Painted Hills Pastry, offering French pastries, cakes, breads and cookies. They have sandwiches, too, if the bacon cheeseburger has worn off.

After lunch, take a stroll through Mitchell. It won't take long, but will deliver many charms. There's the Wheeler County Trading Co., which in typical small-town style attempts to cover a lot of bases all at once. The signs on the old wooden building offer groceries, hardware, sporting goods, antiques and "needful things." Who doesn't need needful things? You'll pass a lodging and souvenir shop, the Little Pine, and then encounter the Oregon Hotel. First established in the 1800s during the gold and early fossil days, the two first versions of this hotel were destroyed by fire before this structure was built in 1938. The stately white building still stands as a quaint and extremely affordable lodging option.

I stayed at the Oregon Hotel in the late 1990s with a group of fellow college students on an exploration of the geology of the area. The rooms are tiny and full of antiques, there is an old-fashioned sitting room, and the overall effect is cozy and charming. The big white building has a comfortable front porch for relaxing and a side yard for more of the same. For me, I just love that this tiny hotel in a tiny town in Eastern Oregon decided to take the title as *the* Oregon Hotel nearly 150 years ago. Why not? Somebody had to do it.

Pretty little Bridge Creek runs right through town. There's a city park at the east end of Main Street, perfect for a peaceful break as you contemplate your day. While you're at it, keep your eye out for bears. Who knows, maybe Henry will come back one day, in search of cookies fed to him by tourists. Then drive back through the forests of the Ochocos towards home.

## *Sidetrip*
## BIG SUMMIT PRAIRIE

Return from Mitchell through Big Summit Prairie for a very scenic drive back to Bend. Take Bridge Creek Road south out of Mitchell and wind through the Ochoco Mountains to emerge in an incredible high desert prairie. Big Summit Prairie is several thousand acres of grassy plain, expansive and lovely, with a creek running through and the occasional majestic ponderosa pine anchoring the meadow. It's the kind of place that is easy to do a little "ooh-ahh" drive-through, but, as always, stopping makes the experience richer. Much of the prairie is privately owned, but pull over to take in the flora and fauna of this amazing prairie from the roadside. Rich earth, water and plenty of sunshine make Big Summit Prairie plant heaven. It is simply teeming with wildflowers in the late spring and summer. Scarlet gilia, shooting stars, mule's ears, paintbrush and lupine are just a few wildflowers you can expect to see, delivering colors from red to yellow to purple. The Prairie is also home to several pairs of summer-nesting sandhill cranes— take the binoculars and keep your eyes peeled for their long elegant frames and graceful gait. I've seen the cranes each summer visit, as well as birds of prey and perhaps deer or elk, as well. Late afternoon to dusk is the best time to drive through here, when temperatures cool and wildlife is more active. You might even catch a spectacular sunset. It's the perfect end to your day trip.

## *Overnighter*
# THE PAINTED HILLS VACATION RENTALS

This is my favorite kind of Oregon story. A mother-daughter team originally from Germany tired of city life and moved to Mitchell. There, they bought two cottages, remodeled them, filled them with artwork created by the father of the family and opened them as vacation rentals. The mother, a master gardener, created a magical garden between the cottages. They had no idea if people would come. They have. The Painted Hills Vacation Rentals are an idyllic, magical place to put up your feet for the night. Awake to the silence and fresh scents of an eastern Oregon morning. Equally awesome in a totally different way is Spoke'n Hostel, a donation-based hostel in an old church that caters to cyclists. A bunk, breakfast and a shower—sometimes that's all you really need.

S

# SOUTH

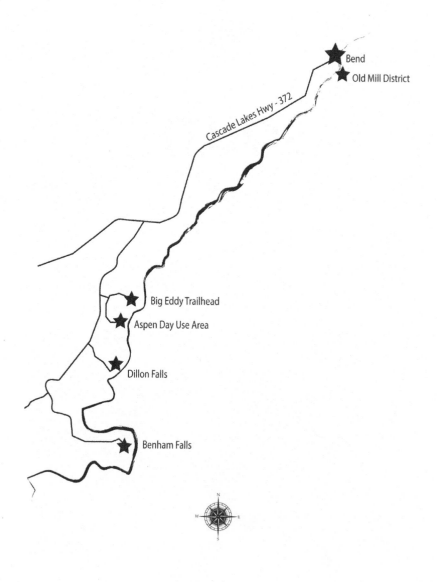

# THE DESCHUTES RIVER TRAIL

## Walking, white water and marshmallows

*Distance: The Dillon Falls parking lot, the farthest destination in this day trip, is 10 miles south and west of Bend.*

A river runs through it. In many ways, the Deschutes River defines Bend. The town wouldn't even be where it is—and what it is—if it weren't for the river. Bend was founded as a timber town and grew up around this waterway, and the river continues to be central to the daily life of the city to this day. Today's day trip is an ode to the Deschutes and experiencing this wonderful river several ways in one day. You're going to be busy and, at least at one point, quite wet.

Start your day in the Old Mill District. Grab a cup of coffee at Strictly Organic Coffee Company in the center of the shops and walk across the street to the footbridge that crosses the Deschutes River. The Old Mill District is now a giant mall (if a lovely one), but its name is accurate—this is the historic site of two lumber mills, Brooks-Scanlon and Shevlin-Hixon, which were the predominant economic engines of early Bend.

The footbridge connecting the Old Mill District shopping and dining center to the Les Schwab Amphitheater is a good place to ponder all of the growth and change that has come to Bend since the city was founded in 1905, if you are so inclined to such pondering. As recently as the late 1990s, this part of town was populated only with tired mill buildings while the riverbanks were trampled and logs floated in the water. People weren't allowed in the river at all back then—it was far too dangerous.

Today, the river at the footbridge is alive with wildlife. Historic signs interpret the past in photos and text, juxtaposed against the landscaped riverbanks and trails teeming with people. Boaters and stand-up paddleboarders pass under the bridge below your feet. Downstream a half mile is a $2 million dollar waterpark, crowded with surfers and floaters all summer season long and even in the off-season. There are 19 miles and counting of riverfront trail to explore in Bend. No matter how you feel about progress, it's hard to deny that the Deschutes River in Bend is more loved and more accessible now than ever before in its history.

After our urban stroll and historical contemplation, we're going to venture south into the national forest to enjoy a wilder, rougher, completely different part of the Deschutes. Pack your comfortable walking shoes, sunscreen, bug spray, food and water—we're going into the woods. Drive from the Old Mill District up Century Drive, as if you're headed for Mt. Bachelor, and watch for signs for Forest Service Road 41, which will be a left turn. This road accesses the river at many points through some of its prettiest sections. It's lovely, forested, somewhat remote and relatively un-crowded. Though fully accessed by trail, with several nearby choices for parking, the river sections here remain light in foot traffic, except for on the busiest summer weekend days.

— There are several different parking and viewing areas along Forest Service 41. In this section we are going to discuss two: Big Eddy and Dillon Falls. The other viewing areas are Lava Island Falls, Aspen, Slough and Benham Falls West and East—the latter of which we access in this book in the Sunriver chapter.

Once you've turned off of Cascade Lakes Highway onto Forest Service 41, look for a turn to the left approximately one mile from the highway, signed as Big Eddy Day-Use Area (you'll need to bring a Northwest Forest Pass or pay $5 for a parking permit at the lot). This is our first stop—here you'll find good parking and a bathroom. Hike upstream just a half-mile on an easy trail and see kayakers and rafters running the Class III Big Eddy falls.

Our next stop is Dillon Falls. Return to Forest Service 41 and take a left. Travel less than a mile to the Dillon Falls sign and turn left into the parking lot. From here, walk a short distance downriver to Dillon Falls—a long, multileveled falls, tumultuous and rocky. It's not like your traditional tall cascade, but more like a short falls followed by a long stretch of big rapids. Because of this, Dillon is still boatable by those who can handle Class V rapids. If you're lucky you'll witness a few kayakers navigate the treacherous waters while you watch safely from shore.

In all cases, you'll be on a single-track dirt trail passing through a gorgeous forest of ponderosa pine, green manzanita and snowbrush. The river is clear and wild here, as opposed to most of what you see in town, where a dam deters flow. It's likely you'll see ducks and birds of prey; deer are commonly sighted. Across the river are glimpses of the chunky a'a lava flows that define this whole area. This section of the river is closer to Newberry Crater than Bend (we learned more about that volcano in previous chapters). The lava flows from the Newberry eruptions shaped the river in this area and still dominate the landscape today. You'll see much more lava than you would in town. I once flew over this area in a helicopter and was struck by how the overhead view was largely snaking fields of black, impenetrable lava.

When you're done exploring the river trail, drive back into town the way you came, to your next destination. Sun Country Tours, headquartered on Century Drive, has the commercial permit to float the Big Eddy section of the Deschutes, and they use it well. Trips depart from their shop many times a day. Make a reservation in advance for an afternoon trip and get ready for some fun.

I lived in Bend for nearly 20 years before I signed up for the three-mile, Big Eddy float with Sun Country Tours. That's something that tourists do, right? Like the Cycle Pub, that bicycle-powered beer-drinking vehicle you see people pedaling around town. But the first time I gave Big Eddy a try, I was surprised to discover that it was a total blast. Short, sweet, and reliably fun and wet, it's a great time for the family. The guides have the experience dialed in—get on the bus, get on the boat, float for an hour, see some wildlife, do some bonding with the others on your boat, end with awesome rapids, get wet, be back in town in time for happy hour. Check!

(By the way, the Cycle Pub is fun too. Who knew?).

Incidentally, if you're paying attention, you'll notice that the shuttle bus trip to the put-in takes you right back up the FS 41 road, which you just drove for your waterfall exploration picnic and hike. From your raft in the water, check out the trail you just hiked.

Once you are back at Sun Country, change into some dry clothes—your river-loving day trip isn't over yet. Next we're going downtown. The Deschutes River is dammed at the Colorado Bridge in downtown Bend, which creates Mirror Pond, Bend's famous front yard and a killer photo opportunity. Stand at the Rademacher House, the long-ago residence of a Bend icon, which is now home to the café and coffee shop The Commons, and take in the view across the water to Middle and North Sister in the distance. You're looking at Drake Park, which runs along the east bank of the river. The park is landscaped with a variety of deciduous trees, many of them very old and established, which makes the view even prettier, especially in fall when the leaves change. Wait until the sun dips low enough in the sky to create that late afternoon, magical light and snap a few pictures. Then wander a block downriver to the Pine Tavern for dinner.

The Pine Tavern restaurant hasn't been around as long as the timber mills were, but it's close. It was founded in 1936, a time when nearly the only people to feed in Bend were timber industry workers and their families. Tourists were few and far between, though the occasional visitor did wander through. During World War II, soldiers stationed at Camp Abbot (mentioned in the Sunriver chapter) would sometimes make their way to Bend and to the Pine Tavern for a meal. Eventually, the tourists and skiers did find Bend, of course, as well as did the extra 100,000 people or so who have moved here since the 1930s. Throughout, the Pine Tavern has been a treasured and classic destination on the Deschutes. Sit outside if the season is right—the landscaped garden is delightful and the view of the river is better from here.

If it's still light and you have energy after dinner, walk north from downtown through Pioneer Park, downriver from the Portland Street bridge. Pioneer Park is one of Bend's oldest—in fact, it used to be a campground hosting the earliest tourists to the area. The river trail from here passes through a very scenic section to what is known as the First Street Rapids, where you might see kayakers at play, birds of prey in flight or the local fire department doing some swift water training. End your day of Deschutes River worship by watching the river continue north and imagining its long journey to the Columbia River.

## *Sidetrip*
## DESCHUTES RIVER TRAIL LOOP

If you don't want to leave Bend but want a quick overview of sections of the Deschutes River Trail both urban and forested, try this accessible loop. This trail can be crowded on a weekend, so maybe choose a weekday. But even crowded, it's a great way to see a beautiful part of the Deschutes right from town. Park in the Old Mill District or one of its parks, Riverbend or Farewell Bend. [Depending on where you park, this loop is about two to four miles total]. Head upriver on the east side of the river. Paved trail through parks and playgrounds will give way to a narrow dirt trail winding through a forest. The river gets more rugged here. The trail travels through varied and lovely terrain, as well as delivers a few terrific overlooks. It crosses the river a mile upstream at a footbridge with views upriver of a stunning narrow canyon section, marked by tumbling rapids and tall pine trees, before returning on the west side back towards the Old Mill District. Keep your eye out for wildlife. From one of the overlooks on the east side, I once saw a man standing on a rock in the middle of the river, absolutely naked and playing a trumpet. But I would say that's uncommon. It's more likely you'll see otters, birds and deer. Make your way back by way of the west side of the Deschutes and reward yourself with a craft beer at one of the Old Mill's many dining establishments. For the sake of everyone else, leave your clothes on and keep the trumpet in the car.

## *Overnighter*
## RIVERFRONT STAYCATION

Many of the waterfront properties close to downtown Bend have converted to vacation rentals in recent years. While this fact may not always be popular with locals, it still means anyone, locals and tourists alike, can take advantage of the opportunity for an awesome staycation on the river. Check vrbo.com for houses to rent in town on the Deschutes, and spend a weekend floating the river, gazing at wildlife, walking to tons of restaurants, shopping and toasting marshmallows over a fire pit in the backyard of your home away from home. You might never want to leave.

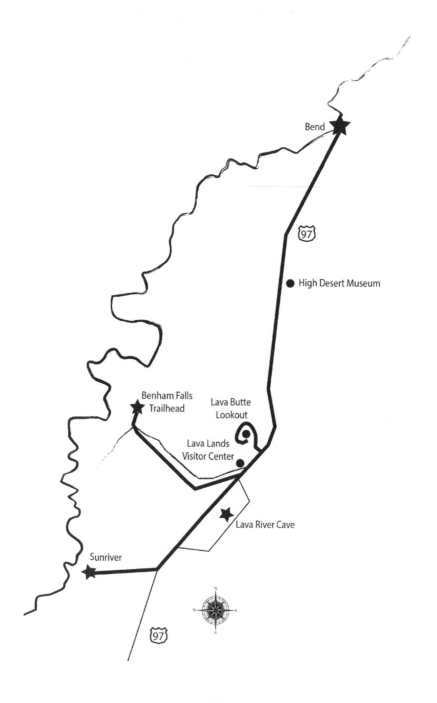

# LAVA LANDS

## Volcanoes, ghost trees and craft beer

*Distance: Lava Cast Forest, the farthest destination in this day trip, is 24 miles south and east of Bend.*

Living in Bend means being surrounded by an epic geological story. Our entire landscape is volcanic, from the Cascade Peaks in the western distance to the rimrock along the Deschutes River to Pilot Butte, the cinder cone right in the middle of town. Nevertheless, the history and origin of the rocks around us is not something most of us think about daily. This day trip is all about learning something about the lava landscape that defines this part of Oregon, and then rewarding yourself at the end of the day with beer and ice cream (the anticipatory payoff for a day of education).

Our first destination is Lava Butte, located right off Highway 97, 10 miles south of Bend. It is adjacent to Lava Lands Visitor Center, and both the butte and the interpretive center are part of the mother ship that encompasses them, Newberry National Volcanic Monument. Newberry Monument was established in 1990 to protect the area around Newberry Crater. The Cascade Range is part of the Pacific Ring of Fire, the volcanoes and subduction zones located around the rim of the Pacific Ocean. All significant, known volcanic eruptions in the contiguous United States have been from the Cascade Range, the most recent and memorable being the eruption of Mount St. Helens in 1980. But many other smaller eruptions outside of the Cascades formed features throughout the region over thousands of years. Newberry Volcano, which is 40 miles east of the main Cascade Range, was last active 1300 years ago, and its activity over time impacted much of our landscape.

In this chapter, we're going to cover the northern half of Newberry Monument. The southern half of the monument, including Newberry Crater itself, is discussed in the Newberry National Monument chapter to come. Pack layered clothing, hiking gear and food for this excursion. There are no food services down this way until you get to Sunriver, so before you leave Bend, grab some sandwiches and other provisions at the Village Baker on Bend's westside or at C.E. Lovejoy's Market on the south end of town for a picnic lunch to consume at some point during the day.

Lava Lands Visitor Center is well signed and easy to access right off Highway 97, and you can drive right to the top of the butte in minutes. Lava Butte is a cinder cone, or volcanic cone. Cinder cones are essentially small volcanoes, formed as lava repeatedly erupts, hardens midair and falls into a growing mound of cinders. The best-known cinder cone in Central Oregon is the aforementioned Pilot Butte, that iconic landmark in the center of Bend, and the only volcano within city limits in Oregon. But Pilot Butte is hardly lonely in the Central Oregon landscape, nor is Lava Butte—there are over 400 volcanic cones in the Newberry National Monument boundaries alone. Most are ignored, practically invisible to those of us who live surrounded by them. Gain some elevation, however, like from an airplane, portions of the Cascade Lakes Highway or the top of 500-foot-tall Lava Butte, and you quickly discern that the ground is speckled with lumps of varying sizes for as far as the eye can see. The effect is as if an enormous blanket has been laid over a field strewn with dozens of bowling balls.

At the summit of Lava Butte, a small viewing hut houses interpretive signs that identify the major buttes, peaks and ridges on the horizon in all directions. From this vantage point, and considering the number of peaks listed, the entire state of Oregon seems to be comprised of volcanoes. Here's where you really begin to discern how our landscape was created. In the distance are stately Mount Hood to the far north to tiny Pilot Butte only a dozen miles away. In between are Mount Washington, Tumalo Mountain, the Three Sisters and more. To the south, visible on the horizon, is striking Mount Thielsen. Also on view is the rim of Crater Lake, created when Mount Mazama blew its top 7700 years ago, leaving a massive crater that would eventually fill with water to become the deepest lake in North America, and, eventually, Oregon's only national park. (Crater Lake is covered in an earlier chapter). Identifying the Crater Lake rim with the help of the mountain peak finder is a cool experience, as it's tough to pick out without navigational guidance. From here you get a sense of the height of the Crater Lake rim, its relative closeness to Bend and its camouflaged nature—you'd have no way of knowing that there's an enormous, cerulean lake behind that rocky ridgeline.

The top of Lava Butte also provides the opportunity to see volcanic material up close. In fact, you can literally stoop to pick up a handful of lava (albeit long-cooled lava, thank goodness). Below your feet are hundreds of rocks—or more accurately in this case, cinders. Cinder cones and their composite parts typically appear to be red from a distance, but the rock up close at the surface varies in color from brown to rust to pink to purple. The kids will love this—when have they ever seen a purple rock? The summit of Lava Butte is also a small caldera, indented in a concave bowl at the top. This is typical of volcanoes, which often settle in the middle during formation (just like Crater Lake, only it's much, much bigger than Lava Butte or most other volcanoes). Take a walk around this caldera, absorbing the 360-degree views as you go.

Also visible from here are many lava flows that cut through the pine forest below, all originating from the Newberry volcano. Newberry represents young volcanic activity, relatively. As I mentioned, Newberry was last active only 1300 years ago. Its offspring are Lava Butte and the Big Obsidian Flow on Paulina

Peak. These formations are 7000 years old and 1300 years old, respectively. In contrast, the volcanoes of the Cascade Range vary in age from 100,000 to 2,000,000 years old.

The relatively new lava surrounding Lava Butte is described by a Hawaiian word, a'a, and is chunky and black, dramatic and off-putting. One look at the rough and jagged landscape and you're sure you won't be taking a walk in it, though in fact you can do just that thanks to a paved walking trail that winds through a short section of the lava in front of the visitors center and includes interpretive signs to help you understand what you see. Inside the visitor center is the opportunity for more learning as well as activities: float pumice rocks in water, see a core soil sample layered with ash falls from the eruptions of Mazama and Mount St. Helens, watch video of a lava flow in action, and peruse a 3-D map of the entire Newberry Volcanic Monument. (The visitor center is only open seasonally, in the warmer months.)

Next up on our rocky day trip discovery is a trip underground. You've seen the lava flows and cinder cones from great heights—now let's take an excursion into the volcano's underbelly by way of Lava River Cave. Newberry is a shield volcano, created by large lava flows of its own origin. Rivers of molten lava flowed sometimes as far as 70 miles from the volcano's center before hardening into basalt. Sometimes the top layer of basalt hardened first, while the hot layer beneath kept flowing out. The result is a tunnel or tube left behind. These are called lava tubes and are one of Newberry's (and Central Oregon's) most fabulous secrets. The largest are essentially elongated caves. The longest in Newberry—in fact the longest known continuous, un-collapsed lava tube in Oregon—is Lava River Cave.

From the Lava Lands Visitors Center, drive south two miles to Lava River Cave (follow signs—it's not on the highway). Just as there are hundreds of cinder cones in Central Oregon, so too are there hundreds of lava tubes. Most, however, are not open to the public. Lava River Cave is, at least seasonally. During the summer season, visitors can walk deep into the cave, seeing stalactites, stalagmites and even the occasional resident bat— though the bats are very shy and seldom seen. (The bats, not the weather or staffing, are what keep the caves closed in the wintertime, for their protection during hibernation, and to prevent the spread of the fatal white-nose syndrome that has afflicted bats in recent years). In case you forgot your high school geology, stalactites are the rocky formations that hang from the cave ceiling, and stalagmites come up from the floor. All year, the cave holds a steady interior temperature of 42 degrees, never varying because of its enclosed, underground environment. Of course, it's dark all year long, too, so bring a jacket and light source for your journey here no matter the outside weather.

If you're like me, just a taste of the cave is enough. It's a mile long, and if you're up for an adventure, navigate the whole thing, crawling through narrow corridors, watching for the sign designating the point at which you pass under Highway 97, looking for mice and encountering a mysterious sand garden. But there are no forced marches or expectations here—you can walk into the cave as short or far a distance as you'd like. If the idea of traipsing deep into the ground is a bit uncomfortable for you, no worries—it's still worth it to take a brief trip into the cave entrance as far as you like. The cool air, strange mineral smells, shadowy walls and magical rocky formations offer a great taste of spelunking, as well as an understanding of the power of lava to carve tunnels underground.

Awaiting us at our next stop, Lava Cast Forest, is another cool feat accomplished by molten lava as it tears across the land. From Lava River Cave, journey another two miles south and then 10 miles east on unpaved Forest Road 9720/950 (both named Lava Cast Forest Road). This destination is pretty much on the way to nowhere down a gravel road, and so maybe is the least visited of the Newberry features. But it's also a place that inspires a significant amount of awe, so it's totally worth the effort to get there. Lava Cast Forest is a little bit difficult to understand until you've seen it, but basically, it's a collection of fossilized trees, or really the fossilized absence of trees. Here's how it works—lava flowed from the northwest flank of Newberry Crater 7000 years ago around a forest of living trees. The hot lava incinerated the tree trunk wood it encountered while simultaneously hardening into a mold of what had been moments before. The last time I was there, my daughter crawled inside a cylindrical tree cast and announced she was standing inside a tree ghost.

An interpretive trail winds past several tree casts, accompanied by a fairly terrible brochure, which interprets this place as even more boring than it maybe already is. All around you, the landscape stretches rocky and mostly treeless for miles. The atmosphere is ascetic, marked by what isn't there. In a way, that's true of all volcanic landscape. There was plenty of drama, once upon a time, but that was so very long ago. Now, all is about as immobile and permanent as is anything in our lifetimes gets. You must imagine the drama, conjure the ghosts, dream up the great story of the volcano in your head.

When you've had enough contemplation about rocks, lava and passing time, throw in the towel and head for the ice cream. Return on the gravel road to Highway 97 and travel south a few miles to Sunriver. After the cold, dark cave and the stark volcanic landscape of lava cast forest, the busy mall at this popular resort community will feel like full-force modernity and sensory overload, especially if it's high season and the visitors are out in full force. But that's okay. Grab the kids an ice cream cone at Goody's Soda Fountain and Candy (they make the ice cream themselves) and let them play on the small playground and play structure in the mall, while the grownups sip a cold Vicious Mosquito IPA on the patio at Sunriver Brewing Co.

For fun and local color, venture to The Mountain Jug, an off-the-beaten-path Sunriver shop with 12 regional craft brews on tap to drink there or take home in a growler. There isn't much in the way of food here, FYI, but other charms prevail. The beer is fresh and new, but the Jug is just as famous for its old-fashioned surprises. Check out their vintage arcade console (isn't it high time you taught the kids to play Donkey Kong or Pacman?), AC/DC pinball machine and catalog of over 1000 vinyl records.

End your day of exploring rocks by, well, rocking.

## *Sidetrip*
## THE HIGH DESERT MUSEUM

I used to work at the High Desert Museum, and marketing was always a bit of a challenge. How can you name a place after a desert and convince people it is interesting? Yet, in fact, the museum is incredibly interesting. There's a lot more going on here than sagebrush. Living history, exhibits covering Native Americans to butterflies to quilts to watersheds to fur trappers, outdoor pathways on which you can see otters, teepees, a homestead and a sawmill, live bats and black widows, and birds of prey prepared to fly over your head for a mouse-treat are just some of the delights of this place. You could easily spend a day here. When you walk through By Hand Through Memory, think about me—in the summer of 1999, I painted the backdrops for the artifact cases, out behind the museum in the summer sunshine. What a great job that was! But I like writing better.

## *Overnighter*

Sunriver is where to stay the night. See the next chapter for more info.

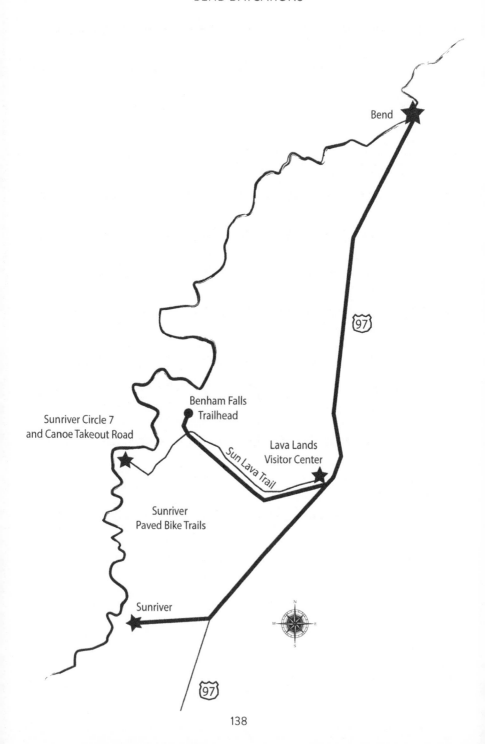

Bend

97

Benham Falls
Trailhead

Sunriver Circle 7
and Canoe Takeout Road

Lava Lands
Visitor Center

Sun Lava Trail

Sunriver
Paved Bike Trails

Sunriver

N
W        E
S

97

# SUNRIVER

## Bike trails, river access and ice cream

*Distance: Sunriver is 17 miles south of Bend.*

It took me until I had kids to understand resorts. Up until then, vacation meant getting away from people— camping, maybe, or choosing a secluded cabin in the woods or a beachfront hotel. But once you're a parent, the whole resort thing comes sharply into focus as the most brilliant idea ever. Restaurants, recreation, cocktails, pools, bike paths, lodging— all in one place? Sign me up. Who cares if there are a bunch of other people there; we all want the same thing, and our kids can play with each other while we drink margaritas.

It was my before-parenting perspective that kept me from appreciating Sunriver for a very long time, even though it was right there all along. The well-established resort community south of Bend was recognized as a top-notch recreational and vacation destination long before Bend rated the same attention. The Sunriver Lodge was built in 1969, when Bend was still a sleepy mill town populated by hardworking loggers, cowboys and a few first-generation ski bums.

Once I realized that resorts rule, it still took me a couple of beats to further understand that I didn't have to be an overnight guest or property owner to enjoy many of Sunriver's amenities. The location on the river, nicely maintained trails and the many services that have sprung up around the resort make it a terrific day trip.

Pack your indoor and outdoor clothes, your swim gear and your bicycles and helmets, and drive 15 miles south on Highway 97 to the Sunriver exit. Grab a map at the kiosk on your way in—at a little pullout on the right, just before the right turn into the business park—and find a parking spot somewhere in the mall. Grab a cup of coffee or a snack at one of the shops. There's a bike shop too if you forgot your gloves or toolkit. Forgot your actual bicycle? Enter benefit number one of day tripping in a resort community—you can rent a bicycle for the day. Benefit number two, three and four—Sunriver has 30 miles of trails, paved and mostly vehicle-free, as well as mapped. You won't fight with cars and you won't get lost (as long as you grabbed that map). This means bicycling in Sunriver is great for the kids, the parents, the newbie or the cautious.

Depending on your cycling team, I suggest making your bike trip into a loop. Sunriver is organized around a series of roundabouts (Sunriver had these before Bend, but they call them traffic circles). Follow the circles sequentially north as far as you wish. Make a pit stop at Fort Rock Park for the playground or the Sunriver Country Store to acquire a beverage. Cut west to the river for the return trip when you've journeyed as far as you wish.

Sunriver is a lovely, forested haven, with plenty of ponderosa and lodgepole pine. The forest is denser on the south end, opening up on the north. The section of trail that follows the river, accessed between circles 5 and 6, is the loveliest. The Deschutes here is wide and lazy, not crashing through canyons as it is in sections north. You'll likely see geese, raptors and jumping trout—maybe deer, heron and otter too. There is a beautiful arched bridge situated near circle 5 that's worth lingering on for views of the river, and the ponds near the Sunriver Nature Center deliver more wildlife sightings.

From the Nature Center, the terrain on this cycling tour opens into meadows, which offer glimpses of the Cascade Range, including Mount Bachelor, Broken Top and the Three Sisters (the latter four slightly hidden behind Tam McArthur

Rim—see the Three Creek Lake chapter for more info on that geological feature). Take the long loop around the meadow (this will add considerable distance) or cut through the meadow on the paved trail back to the Sunriver Lodge for a shorter return. Take a spin past the Great Hall, just south of the lodge, to glimpse Sunriver and Central Oregon history. Before Bend was a hot destination, before Sunriver existed, and before most of us were born, this piece of property was an Army training facility. During World War II, this was Camp Abbot, a place for soldiers to experience a simulated combat environment. Amazingly, the camp only existed for two years before it was abandoned and most of it torn down. Saved was the Officer's Club, now Sunriver's Great Hall, built in 1944. Its construction required ten tons of native volcanic rock and 511 hand-hewn logs from the nearby forest, and the structure was used as a mess hall for only six months before the war ended and it was abandoned. Well, not entirely abandoned—at one point, it was used as a cattle barn. Eventually, Sunriver brought it back to life, and today it is a popular place for meetings, events, weddings and the like.

The Sunriver Lodge was built in 1969 and still stands as the resort's central base. From the Sunriver Lodge and Great Hall (these two places are a short walk apart), you have a couple of choices. Return to the mall and your car, or head for the pool. The Sunriver pool option for regular folks (those of us not living or renting a house in the resort) is SHARC. The $18 million-dollar SHARC facility was built and is operated by the homeowners association, and provides indoor and outdoor pools, a lazy river, water slides and a hot tub (though kids are not allowed in the hot tub, which I am sure makes some people happy and others not-so-much). It's $15 to $25 per person for one day's general admission entry, so be prepared to pony up some cash to enjoy these fancy waters. If you're feeling rich, go for it. Otherwise, spend a little more time hanging out by the river—that's the world's old-fashioned swimming pool, after all.

Now it's time for a beer at the mall! Sunriver Brewing is technically located in a mall (the Village at Sunriver), but it's not Orange Julius. It's a comfortable and classy destination with tasty craft brews and really good food. End your bicycle journey here. Sit on the patio if weather permits—it's small but captures some of the waning sunlight of a summer day, and there is even a very small playground just off the patio for the kids to tackle if they get bored with dinner. If your day trip has been kid-free, I suggest a cocktail on the deck of the Sunriver Lodge as your trip's grand finale. The bar Twisted River Tavern is your source for a margarita or fine Oregon pinot noir, which can be enjoyed indoors, out on the patio or carried down a flight of stairs to a few benches that border the golf course. All venues offer views of the meadow and mountains; watching the sunset from here is divine.

It's tough to choose between Sunriver Brewing and Twisted River Tavern, so I'll throw a third choice at you, that's also kid friendly—Hola! Restaurant, a nouveau Mexican Peruvian restaurant with five locations in Central Oregon. The Sunriver location is in a longstanding restaurant space on a dock at the resort marina, overlooking a side channel of the Deschutes River, far from the mall and housing. The Latin American charm here is enhanced by big picture windows overlooking the water and colorful décor. It's out of the way enough that you can often feel as if you have the place to yourself. The food is excellent, and the margaritas are better, but watch out—one is probably enough unless you want to do the Mexican Hat Dance all the way home. Which, maybe you do, to celebrate the many delights of the modern resort.

## *Sidetrip*
## SUN-LAVA TRAIL *Benham Falls*

The U.S. Forest Service officially opened the Sun-Lava Trail in 2014, a 5.5-mile paved bike path that connects the Lava Lands Visitor Center with Sunriver Resort and the Benham Falls day-use area along the Deschutes River. You can tack some or all of this trail onto the bike loop mentioned above—if you make it as far as Circle 7, continue on to the Sun-Lava Trail. Alternately, park at the trailhead on the far north end of Sunriver and bike from there. This 3.5-mile paved path through the woods travels to the Benham Falls trailhead—from here, it's another half-mile on foot to a gorgeous waterfall on the Deschutes River.

Another popular Sunriver option is a day float of the Deschutes River. Put in at Harpers Bridge on the south end of Sunriver and end at the take-out by the Sun-Lava Trail. Canoes, rafts, kayaks and even standup paddleboards are good choices for traversing this waterway, and all can be rented at the resort. Also, the resort offers a shuttle service to return you upriver after your float.

## *Overnighter*
## SUNRIVER LODGING

This one is easy—Sunriver, of course, is where to stay the night. Rent a condominium, house, or lodge room and experience the modern resort. Enjoy the swimming pools, rental bikes and bike paths, restaurant choices, cocktails, rec rooms and views of the mountains. It's even more indulgent when you're only a few miles from home. Rent a house in the forest or splurge on a romantic lodge room for two. The houses are mostly in the trees and offer more space for your dollar, but few views, given the thickness of the forest. The lodge rooms are more expensive, though with lovely views. You'll feel like you've really gotten away, if only for one night.

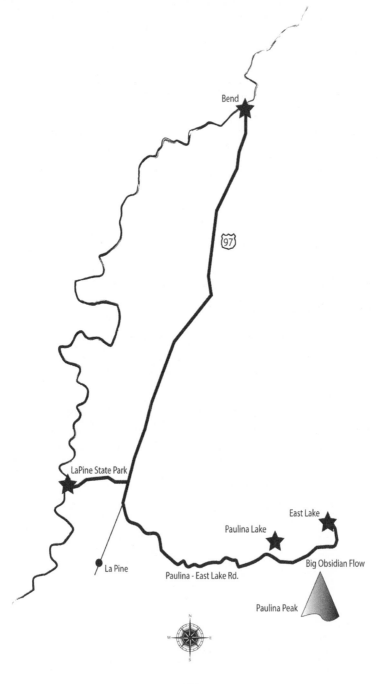

# NEWBERRY NATIONAL MONUMENT

## Obsidian, rocky beaches and taco Tuesday

*Distance: East Lake, the farthest destination in this day trip, is 41 miles south and east of Bend.*

Newberry National Volcanic Monument is comprised of 50,000 acres in all. In the Lava Lands chapter we covered the northern territory: Lava Lands, Lava Butte, Lava River Cave and Lava Cast Forest. Newberry Crater itself, south and east of Bend 20 miles, is the granddaddy (and volcanic origin) of the entire monument. We continue our volcanic discovery of Central Oregon in this chapter, with a day trip to Newberry Crater.

At 20 miles in diameter, Newberry is the biggest volcano in Oregon. It's true! Portland can claim the majestic and famous Mount Hood (Oregon's tallest volcano), but we in Central Oregon have the underappreciated and incredible Newberry Volcano. Newberry also has one of the largest collections of cinder cones, volcanic domes, lava flows and fissures in the entire world. Within its massive crater are many exploration opportunities including two lakes, East and Paulina; Upper and Lower Paulina Creek Falls; an obsidian flow; and the 7985-foot-tall Paulina Peak.

Today's itinerary is for a summer trip. In the winter, the road into Newberry Crater is closed at 10 Mile Snow Park, and the only access is by snowmobile, snow cat or skis, though the Paulina Lake Lodge does stay open for lodging and dining. I skied up there once and found it to be a mostly miserable experience, and long ago gave up that sort of thing for summer adventures. (Notice the significant lack of winter info in this book. If you wanted winter day trips, I apologize. Your guide gave winter up years ago.) The road to Paulina typically opens by May 1 at the very earliest, so plan this trip for summer or early fall.

You'll want to pack a picnic for lunch, though the acquisition of rustic, delicious lake-front dining is slated for later in your Paulina day. Pack outdoor exploration clothes and layers, swimwear and beach gear. Paulina tops out at elevations between 6000 and 8000 feet. The elevation gain means that it's significantly cooler up here than on the high desert floor below. Just as is the case in the mountains and lakes off Cascade Lakes Highway, which we visited in earlier chapters, expect maybe 10 degrees cooler temps on Newberry and, often, breezy days in the summertime. The caldera and its rim also hold snow long after winter, and I've found myself plodding through snow on a June day that was 80 degrees in town, while still comfortably wearing a swimsuit later in the day. Plan for all of the above.

From Bend, head south on Highway 97 23.5 miles, almost to La Pine, then turn left at the signs for Newberry Crater and head 12.9 miles east on National Forest Road 21. The drive east from Highway 97 rises steadily as you climb the mountain's modest but continuous slope. You'll pass by a tollbooth, as there is a fee to enter the monument. (The fee is based on the Northwest Forest Pass, $30 for a year and $5 for a day pass.) This drive feels similar to the climb to Crater Lake or to Timberline Lodge—remote, forested, winding, not many cars and with an anticipatory feel. At some point, you just know, you'll crest a ridge and see something amazing.

That first amazing thing is Paulina Creek Falls, a pair of side-by-side 80-foot waterfalls that pour over volcanic ash flows into a jumble of rocks below. It's a short walk from the parking lot to the falls, and well worth the stop for a moment's photo op. The creek itself is crystal clear, and you can witness the power of water to erode even volcanic rock—many boulders have tumbled from the falls' wall to the pool below.

Next up is a walk through a glittering field of obsidian. As mentioned in the previous chapter, Newberry is the result of relatively young lava flows, 400,000 to 1300 years old. The youngest volcanic formation in the monument, and also the state, is also one of the most amazing to see. The Big Obsidian Flow, at just 1300 years old, is a remarkable cascade of sharp and shiny black rock with a trail through it.

From Paulina Falls, continue past Paulina Lake to the Big Obsidian Flow trailhead. It's a short but somewhat challenging hike from the parking lot through the obsidian—a one-mile loop trail climbs metal stairways and rocky pathways through a landscape of black, sharp and frequently glassy obsidian. You'll definitely want good shoes, and be careful not to trip, or you'll end up with a rock jammed in your palm or a giant scrape up your leg (I might be speaking from experience here). It's a dramatic and lovely pathway made even more so by the contrasting views of Paulina Lake in the near distance and the Cascade Range in the far distance. This is one of my favorite views in Central Oregon—the obsidian, the lake and the mountains from a unique angle are simply awesome. The air is cool, crisp and alpine here, and a single, very persistent pine grows from the top of the lava flow, demonstrating that sometimes Mother Nature reveals her dominance.

Stroll through the obsidian, reach down and touch its smooth surfaces, but don't stick any of it in your pocket, as tempting as all the glass rock around you might be. This is a national monument and no collecting is allowed. I always hand over my cell phone to one of the kids so they can take a million photos, and therefore resist the urge to take home shiny rocks.

Had enough hiking? Let's go to the lake. Newberry Caldera holds two lakes—you already passed Paulina, and now we're heading on to East Lake. Both are popular for fishing, and you'll see boats galore churning their waters in search of trout. It's interesting to note that neither lake had any fish at all until 1912, when both were stocked with fish by the Oregon Game Commission. Rainbow trout were hauled by wagon and bucket to be released in the lake, where they've been happily reproducing ever since.

East Lake is the second lake you'll encounter along the road (there is but one road into Newberry) and our next destination. This lake is large, rocky and somewhat forested; at this elevation and in a volcanic caldera, the landscape is much starker and more exposed than at other Central Oregon lakes you may have visited. Drive to the very east end of East Lake, within the campground, where you'll find a rocky-sand beach good for a picnic and some beach-like play. Set up beach chairs, towels and a few snacks. I usually arrive at the lake thinking I'll be up for a dip, but quickly reconsider. The water, like the lingering snow, is chilly, and the breeze in this high, dry air is pleasant but hints at the potential for a serious post-swim chill. There's often a chop on the lake from the wind, too, and the depth drops off quickly, none of which ever seems to feel overly inviting for swimming once I actually arrive at water's edge.

If your kids are like mine, they prefer other adventures besides swimming, anyway. The rocky beach here is comprised of both grey pumice and red cinders (like those on top of Lava Butte). Invite the kids to conduct a little experiment. What will float? The grey pumice stones, yes; the red cinder, no. It's also common to encounter a passel of frogs at this beach. They are typically sheltered by the dock in a rocky embankment and are tiny—dime-sized—and perfectly camouflaged to the stones. My children spotted them with the eagle-eyes they seem to have for cool things in nature, and immediately corralled a dozen into a small frog pool community.

As for the adults, kick back and take in the view. You can really see the caldera shape from here—it's a perfect bowl around you, lined with huge boulders and some conifer trees.

You can feel the elevation, too. The sun is strong and bright, typically, even on a slightly cloudy day.

If you still have some adventure in you, now's the time to reveal that East Lake has a hot spring, demonstrating that the volcanic origins of Newberry Crater are still, in fact, very active. The hot spring is about a mile and a half walk from East Lake Campground, clockwise, and it's hard to say what shape you'll find it in. The spring comes out of the side of the lake into a rocky lake bank, and usually requires some excavation and shaping to make it dip-able. Despite its unpredictability, the East Lake Hot Springs is one of those legendary, bucket-list-type Central Oregon destinations, so maybe you want to visit just to say that you have.

When you've had your fill of beach time and hot springs, the cooler is empty and the kids are restless, it's time to hit Paulina Lake Lodge for respite and provisions. This retreat attracts families year-round. More wooded and grassy than East Lake, Paulina doesn't have a hot spring but holds its own natural mystery. It's one of the only lakes in the United States to "turn over" periodically. This means an upwelling of water is pushed up from underground through a vent into the lake. The upwelling changes the oxygenation and fish-feeding patterns here, making fishing all the more interesting.

Paulina Lake Lodge offers a handful of rustic cabins, a small store and a modest restaurant. Open for lunch and dinner, the restaurant menu varies from prime rib to taco Tuesday. There's a big open deck—you might even recognize it as one of the filming sites of the film *Wild*. Try to time your trip to catch the lake and dock just before sunset, or the time that photographers like to call "magic hour." The lake is bluer and the sky pinker than at any other time of day. It's romantic and beautiful.

After your fill of tacos and sunsets, descend from the volcano to the high desert floor and head for home, content at a fantastic day spent learning and playing in the volcanic landscape of the high desert.

## *Sidetrip*
# BIG TREE

Want to see a really big tree? Of course you do! Just north of the road that climbs Newberry Crater is the access road to LaPine State Park, west of Highway 97. Here you will find Big Tree, aka Big Red, a 500-year-old ponderosa pine. Big Red is 191 feet tall and 326 inches in circumference. The *Pinus ponderosa* is officially an Oregon Heritage Tree, and the biggest in Oregon, but isn't the biggest of its species. That's because the top snapped off in a storm. Still, it's a beauty, and a massive one at that. Just try to hug this guy. You might have to settle for a kiss.

## *Overnighter*
# LAPINE STATE PARK

LaPine State Park is a truly awesome place to camp. This forest along the Deschutes River is one of Central Oregon's most beautiful and accessible campgrounds. There are traditional campsites, both rustic and deluxe cabins and RV sites, as well as a meeting hall and seasonal park store. Mostly, it's just really pretty here. Kick back and breathe that Central Oregon air, sleep under the stars and fish for trout on the Deschutes. You won't regret it.

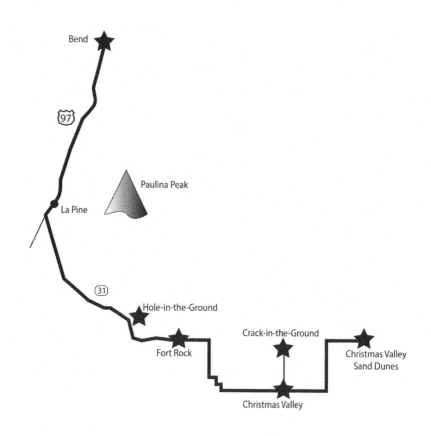

# FORT ROCK

## High desert outposts, geological formations and dunes in the desert

*Distance: Hole in the Ground, the closest destination in this day trip, is 58 miles south of Bend. The Christmas Valley Sand Dunes, the farthest destination in this day trip, is 116 miles south and east of Bend.*

Not that long ago, maybe 50,000 to 100,000 years ago, much of Oregon was underwater. Huge, shallow lakes covered the southeastern part of the state. Some remain—Lake County comes by its name honestly—but even where the lakes are long gone, evidence of them and the volcanism that gave them shape remains. This day trip is about exploring a remote part of the Oregon desert and a few of its geological highlights. We're also going to track down some Oregon quirk and Oregon beer, in that order.

We'll start our tour at a place called Hole in the Ground, which is exactly what it sounds like. But wait—don't leave town for a hole in the ground without provisions. Like several of the journeys in this book, this one ventures out into the wild and rural adventure zone. Today we're going to an area actually named the Oregon Outback, which implies that you will not be finding a GAP or Red Robin out there. Take snacks and water, outdoor clothing and the like. Fill the gas tank. You're going to pass through the city of LaPine, where you should strongly consider grabbing breakfast or lunch at Harvest Depot. Here locals serve homestyle meals in a friendly atmosphere with great service. You'll head off into the desert feeling full in the tummy and more than ready to conquer the outback.

Hole in the Ground is 60 miles south of Bend off Highway 31. Like so much of Oregon, Hole in the Ground's history is all about lava. Between 13,000 and 18,000 years ago, the site of Hole in the Ground was underwater, within one of those lakes mentioned before—Fort Rock Lake. Magma made its way up to the surface near the edge of the lake, blasted the water into steam, and blew out a bunch of rock and soil. This happened more than once; the lake water eventually receded and disappeared, and ultimately what remained was this—a gigantic hole in the ground.

Hole in the Ground is simply a crater in a high desert landscape of sage, juniper and rimrock. While there's nothing inherently fantastic about this place, it still manages to provide a significant awe factor. It's big—a mile across, to be exact—and nearly perfectly round and concave. Walk around the whole thing if you have time. There's no trail, really, just a wander through sage. Stepping through bitterbrush and rabbitbrush begins to get meditative. You begin to get a sense of the desert, its grey-green vistas and wide-open blue sky. For me, it's peaceful, expansive and exposed. Plus, I think it's good for the kids to occasionally lead them on a forced march into the desert to look at rocks and bushes. Hopefully, this gives them perspective and makes them appreciate the pool back home paid for by our HOA dues even more.

Even more amazing than Hole in the Ground is our next destination. Drive south and east 14 miles to Fort Rock, born in the same lake as Hole in the Ground, and also of volcanic origin. You can see what we're heading for from miles away. The immense volcanic tuff ring of Fort Rock is over 4000 feet in diameter and 200 feet high and looks like an indomitable fortress in the desert.

Here's how Fort Rock's volcanic history unfolded. Imagine a champagne fountain at a wedding. The liquid pours up out of a center spout and rains down around the edge. A tuff ring is created in a similar process, only the liquid spouting up and raining down is molten lava and ash and hardens into a ring of rock. Fort Rock was born an island in the lake until the lake became no more. You can still see the erosion rings on the south side of the formation from the lake waves constantly striking the rock.

Okay, but what to do at this huge rock fortress? Walk around and gape. What looked big from a distance is mammoth up close, and the immensity of scale is impressive. Trails and trails-of-use cut through the center of Fort Rock—stroll around and get a good look at the rock up close. If it looks vaguely familiar, maybe it's because Smith Rock, in an earlier chapter, is also comprised of tuff. Both Fort Rock and Smith Rock have that rusty-red-to-brown coloring, which contrasts so nicely with the clear blue sky. Note: pay attention to signs indicating when certain trails are closed to use here, to protect the sensitive environment and wildlife habitat.

Next up is a visit to the modest community of Fort Rock, nearby. You'll find a community church, a grange hall, a restaurant, a tavern and the Fort Rock General Store. The Fort Rock Restaurant and Pub provides the only restaurant food in 50 miles in any direction. Surely, you've worked up an appetite. It's a big flat building in the middle of an even bigger dirt parking lot and serves up the usual rural fare of grilled cheese, burgers, shakes and coffee. There's also a bar serving cold macros and boasting innovative rural Oregon bar art, including pictures of moose, cowboy boots, bears and beer.

If it's open, take a wander through the Fort Rock Valley Historical Homestead Museum, a collection of homestead-era buildings moved from the surrounding area to this site in the 1980s to preserve them from razing or vandalism (admission is $5 adults; $3 children). Buildings include a church, a log cabin, a doctor's office, a school, a land office, and several cabins and houses. It's charming and gives a sense of the homesteaders who once populated this land, dreaming of farms, livestock, independence and financial sustainability. Most of them got the independence and not a lot else in the long run—this land is no good for farming, and ranching works okay, but cattle need more water and food than is easily found out here. (A plaque at Fort Rock reads, "The reason I've been able to produce some fast horses out here is that where I graze them they have to feed at 30 miles an hour to get enough to eat." –Reuben A. Long: lifelong cowboy of the Oregon desert.) Eventually, most of the homesteaders left for greener pastures.

Yearning for a better life in a new place is a theme that underlies much of Central Oregon, in fact, both historically and presently (what do you think has driven the population boom of the last two decades?). This notion is illustrated beautifully in the story of Christmas Valley, our next destination and the location of some of that Oregon quirk I mentioned.

Continue our day trip south and east 30 miles from Fort Rock to Christmas Valley. Originally ranching country, this area received some unlikely attention when it became the site of a real estate scam in the 1960s. In 1961 a land developer laid out a town site, gave it its quirky and euphemistic name, and marketed it to Californians who dreamed of retirement in Oregon or pined for the opportunity to establish their own farm. Penn Phillips may have been a creative salesman, but he was also a liar—he claimed the land was green and great for farming when in fact it's dry, dusty and windy out here. Nor was it quite as picturesque as he declared. That didn't stop Penn from bussing and flying people in for tours, nor did it stop the would-be settlers from buying—the company quickly sold out of all parcels, while promising that the community would soon have more than 5000 residents.

In fact, hardly anyone ever actually moved to Christmas Valley. Eventually, Phillips was sued for misrepresentation. Nevertheless, some folks saw an arid charm in this place, and 1300 people still live here today. As a reminder of the place's storied past, the town retains the street names Holly Street, Mistletoe Road, Snowman Road and Candy Lane—as well as the airstrip, handy if you have your own plane.

Near Christmas Valley is an anomaly even more interesting than a scam artist in the desert, and our next destination. East and north of town is the Christmas Valley Sand Dunes. This chunk of Bureau of Land Management land is 11,000 acres of sand dunes up to 60 feet high, and the largest shifting sand dune system in the Pacific Northwest. Popular with ATV and off-road vehicle enthusiasts year-round, the site also boasts nice views of the south end of Newberry Crater and Paulina Peak. In fact, unsurprisingly, these dunes are also volcanic in origin like so much else around here—they come from ash and pumice from the eruption of Mount Mazama, 7000 years ago, which also formed Crater Lake.

Retrace your steps back to Christmas Valley for an end-of-day meal at the Lakeside Restaurant, Motel and RV Park, for a sloppy Joe, New York steak, or taco salad by the (manmade) lake. Expect a few Oregon craft beers on tap, too—never a bad thing to encounter when out in the wild desert of Oregon, at least in my opinion. Who knows, maybe a beer or two will inspire you to buy a house on Comet or Vixen Street.

## *Sidetrip*
# CRACK IN THE GROUND

Seven miles north of Christmas Valley is Crack in the Ground, a sort of partner geological feature and etymological sister to Hole in the Ground. Out in the middle of the desert is hidden this amazing ravine, a volcanic fissure nearly two miles long and up to 70 feet deep. Normally these kinds of fissures fill in with dirt over time, but because we're in arid, rocky Eastern Oregon, the crack has remained open all these years. A trail runs through its entire length; it is not only a very cool opportunity to hike through a funnel in rock, but also a great chance to cool off in hot summer temperatures, as the bottom of the ravine can be as much as 20 degrees cooler than the outside air.

## *Overnighter*
# THE LODGE AT SUMMER LAKE

The Lodge at Summer Lake is on the north end of Summer Lake, overlooking the wildlife sanctuary. The hotel rooms and cabins are clean and cozy and the Flyway Restaurant is really good. I've had great club sandwiches in their dining room, which has a great view of the high desert, the wetlands of the wildlife sanctuary and the north end of the rimrock of Winter Rim. Bring your fishing pole—the Lodge has a stocked bass pond for fishing. Wake up in the morning to the sounds of migratory birds enjoying the beautiful high desert sunrise on the sanctuary.

# FORT ROCK

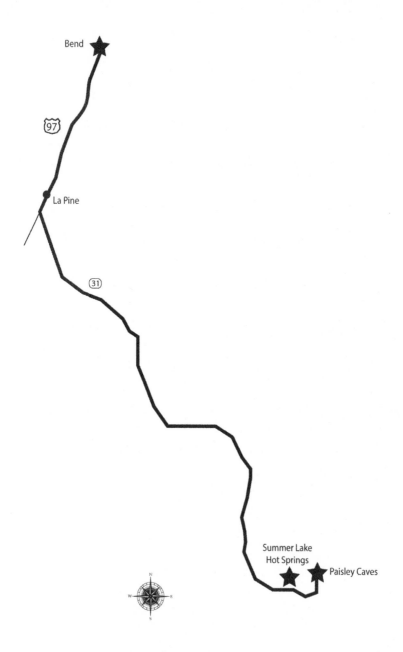

# SUMMER LAKE

## Hot springs, dive bars and a mosquito festival

*Distance: Summer Lake Hot Springs is 124 miles south and east of Bend.*

Give the high desert a fair chance to work its magic, and it surely will. The desert is one of the last best Oregon surprises for many people. Even those who are sure there's nothing out there but sagebrush and sand often find themselves abashed by the experience of a desert journey. I've seen it happen many times. The wide-open skies, expansive vistas and clarifying austerity dig their way into your psyche.

A great place to immerse yourself in the Oregon desert experience is Summer Lake. It's just a couple of hours south of Bend, off Highway 31 in a region known as Oregon's Outback. This trip will reveal petroglyphs, hot springs, dive bars and more before it's complete. I suggest stocking up on road food, water and the like before you leave town. It's remote out here, which is why it's wonderful but also makes it unpredictable in terms of services. I also recommend packing an overnight bag—this day trip is a whole lot better if you make it a two-day trip. And don't forget your swimsuit!

Travel south out of Bend on Highway 97. South of LaPine, Highway 31 tracks southeast into the desert. Immediately, the remoteness of the journey you are embarking on becomes apparent. The road travels through miles of pine forest before emerging into the sagebrush-covered high desert, punctuated with rimrock and the occasional ranch homestead. You'll pass Fort Rock, featured in the previous chapter and clearly visible on the eastern horizon from the highway. You'll zoom through the small town of Silver Lake, noting the small rural-town basics as you pass through: store, church, bar, restaurant, cemetery. Soon enough you'll climb over Picture Rock Pass.

Picture Rock Pass is the high point between the Silver Lake and Summer Lake valleys, on the north end of Winter Rim. Make your first day trip stop here at the top of the pass for an awesome cultural find. On the south side of the highway right at the flat top of the summit are petroglyphs carved into the rocks. Take a little walk and keep your eyes peeled—you'll find the figures of animals and humans clearly visible in the rock. The kids will love this treasure hunt.

From here the highway drops down into the Summer Lake basin. Summer Lake is the alkaline remains of the former Lake Chewaucan, one of the largest water bodies in the region, had you been here 13,000 years ago. This basin is now a flat, bleached expanse, but was once entirely filled with water. One of the driest places in Oregon was once one of the wettest. Remaining in the middle of former Lake Chewaucan is only the tiny pool of Summer Lake. It's barely 15 miles across during its wettest season. From the highway as it descends into the valley, you'll see the lake as a brilliant milky-blue shimmer in the distance.

At the south end of the lake is a hot spring, and our main destination for today. Summer Lake Hot Springs has been a gathering place for hundreds of years. Native peoples established that the springs would be an agreed-upon place of peace for all tribes. It is rumored that U.S. Army Lieutenant John Fremont and his surveying crews stayed at the hot spring for several days on their exploratory trip of the region in the 1840s—though I once received an angry email from a reader saying there was no evidence for this. Whether Fremont actually slept near the hot spring, I can't say for certain, but he did stay in the area long enough to name Summer Lake and Winter Rim. Highway 31, officially installed many decades later, is also named the Fremont Highway.

Today, Summer Lake Hot Springs is a developed place of respite and lodging that remains a destination for desert-lovers and hot springs aficionados from all over the West. Hot, healing waters were, and remain, the draw.

Does anyone remember how a few chapters back I mentioned my love for the modern resort? In Oregon there is a strange phenomenon to look out for. Lots of places call themselves resorts that aren't exactly the four-star, modern luxury resort. You won't be delivered a fresh-made margarita poolside, or cooked a gourmet meal, or cooked anything at all. Some Oregon "resorts" are totally rustic. Summer Lake is one of those (though still hands-down one of my favorite places in the state).

Summer Lake Hot Springs Resort is a smattering of buildings off the south shore of Summer Lake. There are several cabins, a big old bathhouse circa 1928, a glistening playa in the distance and not much else here but high desert and endless sky. The spring reliably delivers 109-degree water into several pools maintained by the property owner, Duane Graham, and his staff. Graham is a former Portlander who decamped to the desert years ago.

With the rental of a cabin or campsite, visitors can access these several hot springs pools (there once was a day-use option and may be once more. Call to inquire). The bathhouse protects the oldest, largest pool. It's timeworn, but marvelous, quirky and charming. The kids will love its warmer-than-usual water, the inlet pipe that dumps nearly too hot water into the pool's edge, and the big white rafters covered with names, carved into the soft wood over the years. Outdoors are several other smaller rock pools, typically a bit hotter than the interior pool, and with the benefit of fresh air and views of the playa and the dramatic 8000-foot Winter Rim, which stretches north for several miles.

Sometimes, especially in inclement weather, the outdoor pools can be chilly, making you want to sink up to your chin to stay out of the cool breeze soaring off the playa. Weather is a significant factor at Summer Lake; the desert is harsh and exposed, and some days, wind, clouds and storms tear over the top of Winter Rim into the playa like gods unleashed. Not that the weather matters all that much when you can witness it from a pool of steaming water. Plus, it's part of the ambiance of the desert. The sky over Summer Lake dominates the senses. It gets into your business, demands that you pay attention. The sky here is huge and blue and full of light—just oceans of incredible light everywhere around you. Photography buffs, take note: it's difficult to take a bad photo here. Everywhere you turn, the view is dramatic and studio-lit. The effect is awesome and relaxing at the same time; I always feel as if my soul has been burned clean under that bright sky.

After your soak, go in search of the labyrinth. My children and I discovered this place accidentally on one Summer Lake stay. Wander downhill towards the playa from the bathhouse, at an angle to the right. Keep your eyes peeled on the ground. You'll come across a labyrinth laid out on the desert floor in rocks. Walk it from one entrance, winding to the middle, and then back out. The kids love this activity, and it's strangely Zen-like. Try it.

If you manage to tear yourself away from the hot springs and the sky and the exploring and the Zen, another adventure awaits you. Climb back in the car and journey nine miles south to Paisley, the closest town to Summer Lake. Your dinner destination is the Pioneer Saloon, which serves as a gathering place for a 50-mile radius. The front of the space is totally family-friendly, albeit there's no mistaking you're in a classic Oregon diner/saloon. Maybe it's the many shelves of liquor on the full-sized wooden bar, maybe it's the crack of the pool sticks hitting balls from the backroom, maybe it's the locals who seem like they live on the stool on which they sit, but you'll know you're in a homegrown watering hole.

All of this somehow makes this place even more fun for both kids and adults. This saloon is relaxed and casual and extremely interesting, with deep history. One wall is covered in historical photos of the area; depicted are plenty of cattle ranching and hunting scenes. A few of the stools around the large communal table are topped with tractor seats, which the kids love. The menu is huge and includes good pizza, standard burgers and the like. You'll even find a craft brew or two on tap, mixed in with the Coors Light and Budweiser.

If you happen to hit Paisley during the last full weekend in July, you're in luck as you've just found yourself at the Mosquito Festival. It involves the usual American festival fun, from a dance to a barbecue to a parade to a quilt show. Even better is the dunk tank and the greased pig contest—the latter only open to children, of course, because obviously adults aren't fun enough to chase after a greased pig.

After dinner, return to Summer Lake Hot Springs and the campsite, cabin or RV site you've rented for the night. The bathhouse is romantic and mysterious in the dark, when soft light illuminates the steam, white walls and crisscrossed rafters overhead. If it's clear, the walk back to your car or cabin afterwards will blow your mind, for the sight of the stars overhead. There's just about zero light pollution out here, and the stars stand out like a million pinpoints of light in a sea of darkness. That desert sky again, gifting us beauty and serenity.

## *Sidetrip*
# THE PAISLEY CAVES

In the right circles, Paisley is very famous, and not for a Mosquito Festival or an ancient, healing hot spring, but for incredible archeological history. Summer Lake's predecessor, Lake Chewaucan, in its 400-acre heyday, was home to many native peoples. Caves at its former southern-most end, very near Summer Lake Hot Springs, are the sites of the oldest definitively dated human presence in North America.

Researchers from the University of Oregon came across this little scientific coup in 2007 by carbon dating fossilized feces, or coprolites, found in the caves. These, dated to 14,300 years ago, are the oldest DNA evidence of human habitation in North America discovered up until now.

The road to the caves cuts north off Highway 31 between Summer Lake Hot Springs and Paisley. As famous and important to science as it may be, there isn't much to see at the Paisley Caves. Follow a dusty, bumpy road through sagebrush that ends abruptly at a massive, concave rimrock wall. You can pick your way through rugged lava rock to climb to the base of the wall and peer into the concave indentations at the base of the rock wall. You won't see much but natural rocky debris, and maybe a lot of packrat poop, but it's still really cool to think that you're witnessing the site where a major scientific discovery occurred.

What is maybe just as good or better is the view from the base of this rock wall. Turn away from the caves and take in the vista. Remember that you are standing at what once was the edge of a great lake. From this perspective on the former banks of Lake Chewaucan, its incredible historic parameters are visible. Before you is a massive basin, its rim hugely vast but still mostly intact, like a gargantuan soup bowl. If you look closely, you can even see wave marks, visible as horizontal swipes through rock. When the wind whipped up across this great lake, the rimrock walls would take a pounding. These eroded sections of rimrock seem to have been made by a large beast that dug its nails into the rock at an exact angle. Gaze at this expanse and ponder the impact of geology, climate and ancient human history before returning to your car, Highway 31 and your journey home.

## *Overnighter*
# SUMMER LAKE HOT SPRINGS

You know you want to—just stay here. Especially since these days an overnight reservation is the only way to enjoy the hot spring waters. There are a few other places to spend a night out this way, but I recommend just holding still at Summer Lake

Hot Springs. There are several weathered ranch houses on the property, originally the only lodgings to rent. More recently, small tiny houses were built. They are creative and charming, with salvaged wood features and floors thermally heated by the springs. Camping is also an option, as are RV hookups. Staying means soaking as many times as you want. Staying means having an extra beer and knowing you don't have to drive anywhere. Staying means watching the kids sink into the place and soak up that desert sky themselves. My kids end up just living in their swimsuits for a couple of days, going back and forth to the guest house as many times as they please. I love watching the sunrise over the playa in the morning from the vantage point of the outdoor soaking pools. The lake lights up blue and the sky comes alive with pink and orange. It's utterly fantastic, and a perfect relaxing send-off to your journey home.

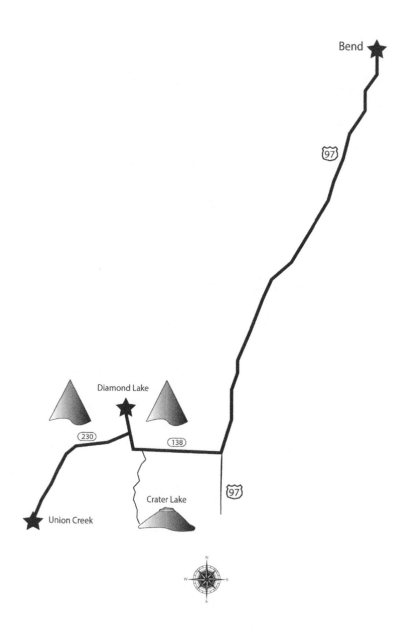

# CRATER LAKE

## Oregon's only national park, acrophobia and a rocker on the porch

*Distance: The north entrance to Crater Lake is 90 miles south and west of Bend.*

I am afraid of Crater Lake. There, I said it. I realize this threatens my status as a native Oregonian and Oregon lover and Oregon travel writer. I can accept that. But you should totally go there. The fact that I'm afraid of Crater Lake is my problem, not yours. What exactly am I afraid of, you ask? Plummeting to my death. But that doesn't really happen at Crater Lake. Really, you should go there. It's awesome.

For a state chock-full of natural wonders, it's amazing that Oregon only has one national park. But Oregon's solo representative makes up for its singularity by being one of the nation's most incredible. Crater Lake, established as a national park by Teddy Roosevelt in 1902, is both a gorgeous destination and an incredible specimen of natural history.

Anyone who has flown over the south-central section of Oregon in an airplane has seen the immense cerulean blue bowl of the lake carved into the earth below. It's so surreal and massive that from the sky one might assume the lake must be visible from most places in the state. But in fact, Crater Lake is remote and sheltered from almost all views, largely because it's inside of a mountain. Long revered by the Native Klamath people, the lake wasn't even discovered by white people until the 1850s, when a few gold miners stumbled upon the rim of this vast blue basin of water. (Stumbled! Ha. They didn't fall in. That doesn't happen at Crater Lake).

Today, getting to Crater Lake by car can still feel like an uncertain venture into the middle of nowhere. The long journey through an uninhabited forest and steep climb up the mountain's flanks reveal little of what is to come. The only hint is the many cars traveling along with you—as the state's only national park, Crater Lake is a popular destination. The good news for those of us who live in Central Oregon is that while the trip can feel remote, in fact the north rim of the lake is only 100 miles from Bend, via Highways 97 and 138. It's an easy and very worthwhile day trip, with a great payoff.

Okay, let's hit the road. We're planning lunch at a restaurant in the national park, so no need to pack a picnic. But lunch might be late afternoon depending on when you leave Bend, so make a pit stop at Market of Choice in Bend or the Sunriver Country Store for some road snacks and drinks, then head south on Highway 97.

As we journey, let's talk geology, or more specifically, volcanism. As has been mentioned many times in this book, much of Oregon is shaped by a volcanic past, and Crater Lake is a prime example. Mount Mazama is a huge stratovolcano in the central Cascades, one of many in a great string of volcanoes running through Washington, Oregon and California. Mount Mazama exploded magnificently 7700 years ago, in an eruption 42 times greater than that of Mount St. Helens in 1980. Rock and lava collapsed into the mountain's center, creating a massive caldera in place of what had been a 12,000-foot peak. This caldera, or volcanic cauldron, filled with rain and snow over centuries to become Crater Lake.

Crater Lake is the deepest lake in the United States and the second deepest in North America, with a depth reaching nearly 2000 feet. The lake is also unique in that it has no inlet or outlet—all of its water is from precipitation, accumulated over time. This means the water is very pure; it's one of the cleanest water bodies on the planet. The purity plus the lake's incredible depth account for its color. Crater Lake appears a very perfect, sapphire blue—the aesthetic quality the lake is so famous for.

Incidentally, it was the hiking and climbing club The Mazamas that named Mount Mazama in the late 1800s, when they made a pilgrimage to Crater Lake. (They also didn't fall in.)

The quickest access to Crater Lake from Bend, meaning from the north, is via the North Entrance, off Highway 138. This day trip is a summer trip—be aware that the ten-mile north-entrance road to the rim is plowed seasonally, usually opening in June and closing in November, depending on snowfall (the south entrance is open year-round). The park is open year-round and people do visit in winter, but the 44 annual feet of snow that falls on Crater Lake mean that winter visitors mostly arrive on skis, snowmobiles or snowshoes. The road trip described here is intended for summer travel when all of the roads are clear of snow and open to cars.

As soon as you climb the north flank of the caldera and reach the North Junction, you'll get your first awesome glimpse of the six-mile-wide lake. (If you're me, now is when you start sweating in the certainty that you're about to drive off the cliff). It's big and blue and will knock your socks off, but don't plan on putting those bare toes in the water just yet. Because of the steep walls of the caldera, there's only one place to access the lake itself—Cleetwood Cove—and that's where we're going to begin our journey.

Drive east from the North Junction on Rim Drive to the Cleetwood Cove Trail. This steep, dusty and challenging one-mile trail is the only access point to the lake itself and is also the launch site for boat tours to Wizard Island. This little island erupted into being a few hundred years after Mazama's main eruption, along with other cinder cones not tall enough to breach the water's current surface level. Several times a day, depending on the season, boats shuttle guests out to Wizard Island, a volcano within a lake within a volcano. Make a reservation in advance for this cool tour. It's awesome to be on the lake itself and then set foot on the tongues of lava that extend around the main cinder cone of Wizard Island. If you are feeling ambitious, hike to the island summit to check out the volcanic vent known as the Witches Cauldron.

After your boat journey, it's time to drive to lunch at Crater Lake Lodge. Most of the park's services are on the south rim of the lake, including park headquarters, both visitors' centers, both campgrounds and Crater Lake Lodge. From Cleetwood Cove, travel the east rim to the Lodge (either direction works just fine, but for this day trip we're planning to travel the entire rim drive, beginning on the east rim and returning on the west rim). As you drive around the rim, expect to see a marvelous view of the lake from several angles. Get out of your car at a couple of overlooks to take in the epic view (while worrying desperately about falling in, and occasionally lurching urgently at the children to grab the back of their clothing in terror) before continuing to Crater Lake Lodge.

It's amazing that Crater Lake Lodge even exists. This magnificent old lodge is perched 1000 feet above the edge of the nation's deepest lake, with 2000-foot rim peaks surrounding it, in a rugged alpine landscape, in a place that gets an average of 44 feet of snow annually, and still somehow was built over 100 years ago before there were even decent roads, let alone semi-trucks.

Crater Lake Lodge was built in 1915 with much difficulty, thereby creating one of the West's greatest "little engine that could" stories. The lodge suffered much during the Great Depression when visitation dropped off significantly, was closed entirely during World War II, and closed again for what seemed like for good in the late 1980s when the park service deemed the deteriorating building unsafe.

Crater Lake Lodge was scheduled for demolition, but the public objected, and eventually a $15 million dollar renovation was completed, reopening the majestic lodge to the public in 1995. You can stay here overnight, of course, but reservations are hard to come by. Lunch will do for us on this day trip. You may have to wait a bit for a table, especially if it's a busy summer day, but it's worth it. The dining room is magnificent, with walls of flagstone and pine, tables covered in white linen, a fireplace anchoring one wall and another that is a bank of windows with the best view you'll enjoy with a meal all year.

The food is Pacific Northwest cuisine, from pan-seared trout to bison chili. I am particularly fond of their clam chowder. My kids love this place too—it's one of their doses of fancy dining for the year (yes, I do take them to Crater Lake, despite my terror).

You might expect, given the remoteness and class of the place, that lunch at Crater Lake Lodge would be expensive, but it's not that bad at lunchtime. You might even get some entertainment—the staff carry the food out on enormous trays, and I once watched a young man drop an entire tray with many plates into the fireplace. I felt bad for him, but it was quite the spectacular crashing display, and took my mind off of my fears of death for just a tiny, noisy moment.

Out in front of the lodge is an expansive patio with a row of rocking chairs, perfect for taking in that amazing view of Oregon's crown jewel. If there is one available, rest a spell after lunch. Maybe you will meet other visitors and share a few stories, like the one I heard when I was there. Did you know, a few years ago, a Volkswagen Passat rolled over the edge of Crater Lake and plummeted over 1000 feet to the waterline? Completely insane. (See, that does happen at Crater Lake! All my fears have suddenly been justified.)

After your rocking chair moment, stroll the pathways along the rim, looking for ground squirrels and birds as well as those amazing views of the lake (cling to your husband's hand like a desperate crazy person). Head back north, traveling around the west rim this time, and return home, where it's nice and flat.

## *Sidetrip*
## DIAMOND LAKE

While only 20 miles away, Diamond Lake doesn't have much in common with its classy big sister Crater Lake. It's a different world entirely, a little bit more "rural Oregon," with rustic accommodations, guests dressed in camouflage, stocked trout fishing, snowmobiling and snow tubing in winter, and a menu that features something called an Econo Dog. But it can be a fun family destination, with bumper boats, paddleboats and patio boats for rent, horseback riding and low-rent good times. It's worth a drive-through on the way home to see if it's your style. If it is, grab a cabin or a campsite and stay awhile.

## *Overnighter*
## UNION CREEK RESORT

Step back in time for a romantic, rustic stay in the woods at Union Creek Resort. This place has been here since the 1920s and it feels like it, in all the best ways. These cabins and lodge rooms are in the incredibly diverse and beautiful woods of Southern Oregon, along the amazing Rogue River. Onsite is a delicious classic diner named Beckie's, with huge wooden tables and a dozen kinds of pie. The Resort also has an ice cream shop that feels straight out of 1950. Take your ice cream cone for a walk along the Rogue Gorge while you are here—it's amazing. Nearby are several waterfalls and hikes worth exploring too.

# CRATER LAKE

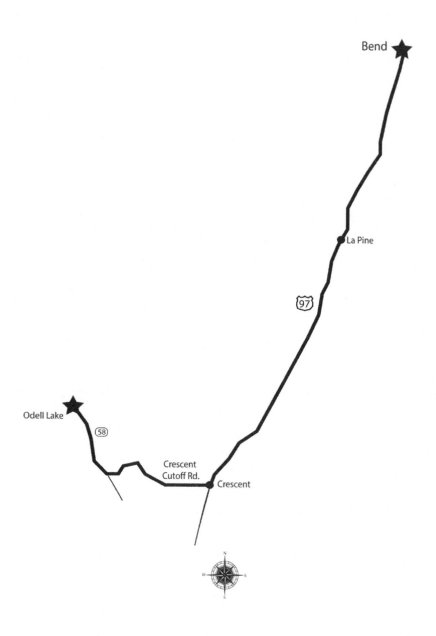

# ODELL LAKE

## A waterfall, a kokanee and a 115-year-old fireplace

*Odell Lake is 67 miles south and west of Bend via Highway 97 and Highway 58*

When I was a child growing up on the Southern Oregon Coast, Odell Lake was where I first tasted snow. Craving a getaway from the blustery wintertime coast in search of a classic snowy holiday experience, my family drove from the rainy ocean to the frosty Cascades on Highway 58 for a long weekend at a classic old lodge.

I remember the crisp, pine-scented smell of the snow, the chill that seeped through my cotton clothing, the white landscape through the antique windows, the wood smoke from the crackling fire in the huge stone fireplace and struggling with the spring-hinged metal bindings on my first (rented) pair of cross country skis.

The lake itself was memorable, too. Oregon has oodles of lakes, and many are featured in this book. But Odell Lake is truly one of my favorites. It's a little bit special for several reasons, including depth, altitude, the train that passes by, the kokanee that lives and spawns here, and one of the oldest lodges in Oregon.

For this day trip, pack clothing layers, water, snacks and good hiking shoes. From Bend, head south on Highway 97. South of LaPine 17 miles, enter Crescent, a very small town packed full of some awesome Americana and visual treats.

Begin by taking in the bigger-than-life bear that perches atop the sporting goods store. He's holding a fish and looks angry, but don't worry, he can't get you, especially if you drive right on by. If you do stop in, the store under the bear offers a nice selection of liquor, guns and ammo, should those items be on your shopping list for today.

If you've left Bend without breakfast, pull in to KJ's Café, not too far past the bear. This is the kind of humble, friendly place you know I have a soft spot for—the kind of place where you can get a gigantic omelet, a postcard and a pair of socks all at once. An old-fashioned Formica counter is the place to sit for reliable diner food, and plenty of it. You won't go away hungry.

Another option is Bigfoot Tavern. You may find it to be a bit early in our day trip to step inside this bar, so maybe just snap a photo of Bigfoot himself, life-sized, carved from wood and guarding the front door.

When you've had your fill of Crescent, look for signs for the Crescent Cutoff, or Highway 61, which connects Highway 97 and Highway 58 in a 12-mile road that is a classic locals' shortcut. The cutoff is narrower and more winding than the main highways but is a more direct route and will save you some drive time en route to Odell Lake.

Crescent Cutoff is also worth driving for a very cool natural feature of note. About six miles west of Crescent, keep a lookout for an unexpected and impressive glimpse of utterly authentic high desert lava. You're driving through a typical thick lodgepole pine forest when suddenly, mounds of black spiky lava appear to the right. A little research reveals that the source is Black Rock Butte—a small (currently dormant) volcano nearby, and yet another reminder that everything around us in Central Oregon is volcanic.

A couple of miles later, about three-quarters of the way across the cutoff, you'll come across the very southern end of the Cascades Lakes Scenic Byway, where it terminates. Cascade Lakes Scenic Byway, or Highway 46, is the lovely road covered in this book's chapter of the same name. If you are feeling ambitious later in this day trip, and it's the right season, you could return to Bend via Cascade Lakes Highway, passing a string of lovely lakes and mountains. (Keep that in mind that the Byway is seasonal—usually open late May through late October.)

Highway 61 terminates at Highway 58. Drive north for just a few miles and you'll see the blue stretch of Odell Lake appear to your left. Keep your eyes open for a great view of Diamond Peak that appears midway along the lake. Be smart and pull over to properly take in the sight of this nearly 9000-foot shield volcano rather than swiveling your head madly while still in a moving car (speaking from no particular experience).

We are going to blast by Odell Lake for now, however, to continue on to one of Oregon's most awesome waterfalls. About seven miles past Odell Lake is Salt Creek Falls. Easily rivaling the waterfalls of the Columbia Gorge, as well as those covered in this book's North Umpqua chapter, Salt Creek is Oregon's third-highest falls, at 286-feet. (For the curious: first is Multnomah Falls, and second is Watson Falls, in the Umpqua corridor).

The falls is signed from the highway and easily accessed by a short hike to an overlook that perches directly over the falls' drop point. Peer through a sturdy wooden fence straight down a sheer vertical wall of columnar basalt nearly three hundred feet into the pool below, watching the churning water splash and plummet past lush green foliage.

Y'all are well acquainted with my fear of heights at this point, so will not be surprised that despite the fact that the wooden fence is totally sturdy, here is where my hands start sweating and I start clutching at my children's clothing and repeating "be careful," despite myself. Still, this waterfall is way too awesome to miss and I always stop when I'm in the area, sweating hands to be overcome. If you're up for it, hike the trail that winds down the steep hill nearly to the creek below, where picnic tables allow for a snack with a view. Mind signage about staying on the trail and not putting yourself at risk, or trampling the native vegetation and upsetting the wildlife. All of the terrain here is incredibly rugged, with hilly vistas into the thick forest of hemlock, pine and alder.

Return the way you came on Highway 58 to Odell Lake, named in 1865 for William Odell, while the future Oregon Surveyor General was scouting the route that would one day become Highway 58.

Let's begin our time at Odell Lake at Shelter Cove Resort, on the lake's northwest end. Odell Lake is six miles long and one mile wide, and here we're on the eastern flanks of the Cascade Range. Odell's basin was originally carved out by a glacier, west to east. The terminal moraine created by the glacier's movement holds steady on the lake's east end (we'll visit there later), naturally holding water and creating a long, narrow lake.

Shelter Cove Resort sits on Odell Lake at Trapper Creek, which feeds the lake from the northwest. Trapper Creek is a pretty little stream worth visiting all year long, but if you're visiting in early October through early November, you're in for a real treat. The fall is when kokanee spawn in Trapper Creek.

I took my family to Trapper Creek one autumn a few years ago. On the way, I told my girls we were going to see the salmon spawning. "Is that giving birth?" asked the 10-year-old.

"No," replied the 12-year-old, wiggling her eyebrows mischievously. "It's the shimmy-shimmy-ay."

The "shimmy-shimmy-ay" is either a technical scientific term or seventh-grade hallway talk, you decide. (Actual technical scientific definition: to spawn: release or deliver eggs.) But the sight of the kokanee spawning is amazing, and probably does deserve its own disco-esque lingo.

Park at Shelter Cove Resort and take the short walk west to Trapper Creek. There are two campgrounds here—meander through the sites to find the trail along the creek. A wooden bridge doubles as a creek crossing and a great viewpoint. Kokanee are landlocked versions of the sockeye salmon. Unlike their ocean-going brethren, kokanee spend their entire lives in freshwater—in this case, in Odell Lake—and only travel a short distance upstream to spawn.

While spawning, the backs of kokanee salmon turn a vibrant, glistening red. This is part of the spectacle—during high spawning season, hundreds of wiggling red fish swim side by side in the shallow creek, very visible from shore.

The other part of the spectacle is the birds. The presence of so many fish in one place attracts eagles: dozens and dozens of bald eagles who know a free lunch when they see one. Eagles, as predators, don't usually travel in packs, but this density of fish and place brings them together. It can be quite a display to watch the birds of prey hover and dive for a meal.

While at Trapper Creek, take in the forest around you. Because Odell Lake is close to the summit of the Cascade Range, the forest here is more like an Oregon westside forest than it is Bend's own dry eastside forests. Here, it's lush and green and diverse. But Odell Lake sits at an altitude of nearly 5000 feet, and therefore, the forest here is also alpine.

Instead of the Ponderosa pine and juniper that dominate our eastside forests, and the Douglas fir and rhododendron found thick in westside forests, at Odell you'll find mountain hemlock and spruce trees. The underbrush consists of Prince's pine, twinflower, huckleberry and much more.

What's that sound coming down the canyon? Now must be time to talk about the train. Construction began in 1905 on the Pengra Pass rail route, also known as the Cascade Line, which was completed in the mid-1920s and connected Eugene with Klamath Falls. The Union Pacific line is still intact today and is traveled by Amtrak. The route is an amazing way to see the Cascades, with 22 tunnels, multiple bridges across canyons and views of streams and waterfalls in the Douglas fir forest. At many locations, the track runs atop the steep southern slopes of the Salt Creek canyon. The trains echo in the canyon from miles away, thundering past Odell Lake in calamitous climax several times a day. You'll know it's there.

Shelter Cove is a great place to have lunch. Depending on the time of year, eat outside under the summer sun or the winter heat lamps. See those vertical paths cut down the slope directly across the lake from the dock? That's Willamette Pass Ski Area, open in the wintertime for modest Oregon downhill skiing.

The little Hook and Talon restaurant and store has a well-rounded menu (my daughter had a corn dog; me, a club wrap) and fishing shop. When we were there, we rented a boat and went out on the lake. Odell seems a lot bigger, as well as a lot windier, when you are out on the water (it's a little bit famous for wind around here). We threw a few lines in, but no luck catching a kokanee or trout for ourselves, despite hearing that Odell holds the crown as the place where the last two state-record trout were caught. Even fishless, there is nothing like traversing a lake and see the sights of the shore from the water.

The day is waning, now, but we have a historic lodge to visit before we call this day trip complete. Odell Lake Lodge is the old lodge of my childhood memories, that thick-beamed structure with tiny rooms for rent and a massive old stone fireplace. The Lodge is located on the southeast end of the lake and was constructed in 1903. For some context about that particular date and old Oregon lodges, consider this: Crater Lake Lodge was built in 1915, Oregon Caves Chateau opened in 1934, and Timberline Lodge was dedicated in 1937. Odell Lake Lodge is the king of the grandpas.

Stomp up two risers of thick, worn steps to enter the lodge through the gigantic heavy wooden slab of a door, and you'll feel the age of the building. Inside, to the right, the fireplace room is dark and cozy, with views of the lake through very old, thick-paned windows, and of Odell Creek, the lake's outflow. On the wall, a very cool 3-D topographical map illustrates the region nicely. Shelves hold old books and games. A nook across the entry way offers cross-country skis for rent, maps for sale and tee-shirts to take home. Climb the lodge stairs to peer down the time-worn hallway and get a glimpse of the rooms we stayed in those years ago.

Drive home with old trains and older lodges on your mind.

## *Sidetrip*
# CRESCENT LAKE

A near-by option with similar appeal is Crescent Lake, accessed off Highway 58 just south of Odell Lake. Here you'll also find fishing, camping, cabins, a restaurant and a small store. Crescent has a sandy beach or two—something you won't find on Odell. The lake is dammed, which means the water is siphoned off for irrigation and the water level sinks over the course of the summer. Visit early in the summer season for best results.

## *Overnighter*

The old lodge at Odell beckons with the weight of time, but Shelter Cove is my pick for where to stay. We opted for a large three-bedroom lodge unit, with high ceilings, log beds, and incredible views of the lake. The time of year was fall, and the air was crisp and clear. The sunrises and sunsets on the lake are drop-dead amazing, especially if the fog has rolled in to cover the water in a romantic layer of mystery. A pack of friendly ducks were always happy to see my daughters, who themselves found they couldn't resist walking down the length of our personal dock to greet the ducks over and over again. At night, the train howls through in the dark, adding its song to the magical, sleepy forest.

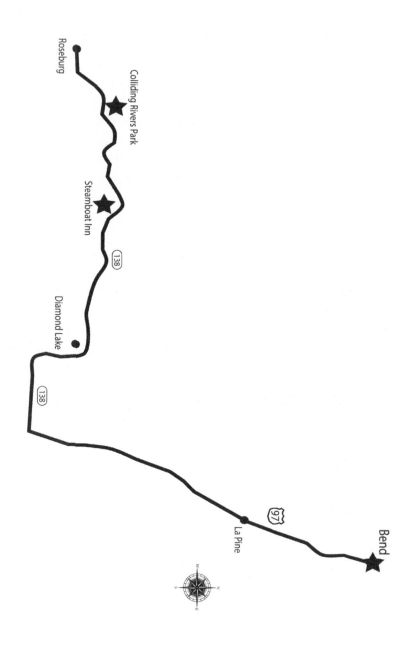

# NORTH UMPQUA

## Waterfalls, fishing holes and river trails

*Distance: Steamboat Inn, the farthest destination in this day trip, is 137 miles south and west of Bend.*

O regon amazes me. Just when I think I've seen every gorgeous wonder in this incredible state, I happen along a place that takes my breath away all over again. A place that still flies a little under the radar is the North Umpqua River. It's remote and far from urban centers. I've lived in Oregon my whole life and had heard Umpqua lore but didn't stumble upon the river's charms myself until I was in my 40s. The North Umpqua is just over two hours from Bend and an incredible destination, especially if you love lush green forests, quiet trails and waterfall after gorgeous waterfall. It's every bit as gorgeous as other Oregon rivers that get more press, like the McKenzie or the Santiam, but far less likely to be overrun with humanity.

From Bend, pack your day tripping supplies. You'll need hiking gear, layers of clothing, and some food, but no need for lunch as that's in the works. Head south on Highway 97. Highway 138 cuts west at the Diamond Lake cutoff, traveling past that lake to intersect with the upper reaches of the Umpqua River. This river flows from here through a section of the Old Cascades between Diamond Lake and Roseburg, and on to the Oregon Coast to join the Pacific Ocean near Reedsport. This day trip stays well east of I-5, focusing on the upper part of the river, which flows through a gorgeous basalt canyon and a thick Western Oregon forest.

Nowhere else in Oregon will you encounter the number and beauty of the waterfalls found on the North Umpqua and its tributary creeks. More famous is the Historic Columbia River Highway west of Portland in the Columbia Gorge, which has six wonderful and popular waterfalls. These waterfalls are as crowded as they are gorgeous and accessible. You might have to travel a bit further to reach the woods of Southern Oregon along the Umpqua, and you might have to search a bit harder for the waterfalls, but you'll find a whopping 17 to feast your eyes upon, and it's a very rare day if you're sharing them with a crowd.

Traveling on Highway 138 from the east, Watson Falls will be one of the first waterfalls you will encounter. Located just south of Highway 138 before Clearwater Lake, this majestic waterfall is the highest in southwest Oregon, plunging 272 feet over the edge of a basalt lava flow straight down into a pool below. The falls are visible from the parking area, or you can get a great view from a wooden bridge that crosses Watson Creek, not far from the parking lot and trailhead.

Just past Clearwater Lake on Highway 138 is Toketee Falls. When I glimpsed Toketee, only the second of the Umpqua waterfalls I would see that day, I was already in jaw-dropped awe. World-famous Multnomah Falls is great, don't get me wrong, but I think I'd put Toketee Falls on my Oregon bucket list recommendations first. It's a true stunner.

Toketee is only accessed by a rugged trail through an old-growth forest along a portion of the North Umpqua River; here water tumbles rambunctiously through a narrow gorge and is part of the show before you even get to the waterfall. A few flights of steps put you in prime viewing position, perched on a cliff wall on a sturdy deck overlooking the two-tiered falls and a pool. The upper descent drops 40 feet, and the lower falls plunge 80 feet over a sheer wall of volcanic basalt. The rock surrounding the falls is as striking and beautiful as the cascade, with a volcanic, striated appearance and green vegetation growing here and there. The word "toketee" means pretty or graceful in the Chinook Native American language, an appropriate notion for this blow-your-mind gorgeous falls.

After Toketee, it's time for lunch, as well as a visit to the venerable and renowned Steamboat Inn. Perched high on the banks of the North Umpqua at a bend in the river is this beautiful lodging. It's also the longtime site of incredible fly-fishing opportunities; fly fishing camps first appeared here in the 1920s. The catch of the day was summer steelhead, and that fish is still the sought-after and difficult-to-catch objective for anglers here today. The Steamboat Inn came to be in the late 1950s, offering lodging and "fisherman's dinners" for the anglers drawn to the beautiful area. You'll love the rustic atmosphere and the great food, served on long plank tables in a classic old lodge dining room.

From Steamboat Inn, head upstream on Steamboat Creek for another waterfall, but first, a very fascinating surprise. Not all of the anglers on the Umpqua historically were willing to display the patience and skill necessary to fly fish for steelhead. Some just took a stick of dynamite to the Big Bend Pool on Steamboat Creek and laid siege to hundreds of native steelhead all at once. Of course, this was illegal, but when has that ever stopped everybody? The steelhead had taken refuge in the cool of the pool from the heat of the summer while waiting for fall rains to send them to their spawning grounds. Some years, the poachers who hit the "dynamite hole" decimated the entire population of fish before they had a chance to spawn.

Enter Lee Spencer, conservationist and FishWatch caretaker, who now camps at Big Bend Pool in an Airstream trailer year after year, to protect the fish. He's a quiet guy, but very knowledgeable about the fishing and region, and happy to educate folks. Big Bend Pool is located about 10 miles up from the Steamboat Inn on Steamboat Creek Road. It's a serene, beautiful and inspiring place to visit. A few miles beyond, find Steelhead Falls, another Umpqua Valley beauty. From there, return to Highway 138. It's time for a hike.

Just as the waterfalls here cast a shadow on those of the Columbia Gorge, so does the Umpqua River Trail outdo its more popular sister, the McKenzie River Trail. The Umpqua River Trail is 78 miles of single-track, riverfront trail through lush forest. There are multiple trailheads, and the trail is broken into 11 sections, so you can easily choose a short or long section to hike. (Unless you are feeling really brave, don't select the 13-mile section rated "difficult" and named "Dread and Terror"—the name says it all). I suggest the Marsters Segment, which is 3.7 miles one way and offers views of the river, old-growth Douglas-fir, and wildflowers, on moderate terrain.

From here, the choice is yours: continue west for more waterfalls or return east for more waterfalls. I won't list all the waterfalls here, though there are many more. One highlight is Fall Creek Falls, accessed by a one-mile, moderately difficult trail. It passes through a narrow, lushly vegetated crevice to become a double falls. Another is Susan Creek Falls, which stands out not only for its spectacular fan over mossy cliffs, but also for what can be found nearby: the Susan Creek Indian Mounds, where Native American boys historically made a pile of rocks to sleep next to overnight, awaiting a vision from their guardian spirit.

If you arrive at Susan Creek and find that you're feeling sleepy, perhaps it isn't due to a full day in the gorgeous Oregon woods, lulled by the sights and sounds of waterfalls. Maybe it's your personal spirit knocking, with a message just for you.

## *Sidetrip*
# COLLIDING RIVERS

Downstream on the Umpqua, near Glide, is a natural phenomenon called the Colliding Rivers. Here, the North Umpqua meets the Little River at a nearly head-on angle. It's the only place in Oregon like it. The water gets all tangled up on itself for a moment before the Little River acquiesces to the powers of the North Umpqua, and the Umpqua continues on towards the sea.

## *Overnighter*
# STEAMBOAT INN

There's always camping, of course, and the North Umpqua has many great choices, including Boulder Flat, Horseshoe Bend and Bogus Creek. But if you're up for a splurge, I suggest a night at the Steamboat Inn. Many of the rooms are fronted by a large wooden deck and walkway, which hangs over the river under a canopy of trees. It's the perfect place to sit a spell and read a book, or forget to read a book because you're too busy taking in the enchanting surroundings. Simply gaze at the river as it makes its way around the bend. The rooms are small and nothing too fancy, but you'll sleep well listening to the tinkling sounds of the river. Guests of the Inn are also privy to a private dinner, in the style of the fisherman's dinner of North Umpqua River lore. It's always gourmet and is said to nurture long conversations and new friendships.

# ABOUT THE AUTHOR

Fifth-generation Oregonian Kim Cooper Findling is an award-winning essayist, writer, editor and author of many books about her beloved home state. She is the editor of *Bend Magazine* and the publisher of Dancing Moon Press. She is the author of *The Sixth Storm*, with Libby Findling; *Bad Mommy Bad Writer: Writing From Home While Keeping the Kids Alive; Day Trips to the Oregon Coast: Getaway Ideas for the Local Traveler; Bend, Oregon Daycations: Day Trips for Curious Families; Day Trips from Portland: Getaway Ideas for the Local Traveler;* and *Chance of Sun: An Oregon Memoir.* She revised the most recent editions of *Scenic Driving Oregon* and *Oregon Off the Beaten Path.* She lives in Bend, Oregon with her family. See kimcooperfindling.com.